DILTHEY'S DREAM

ESSAYS ON HUMAN NATURE AND CULTURE

DILTHEY'S DREAM

ESSAYS ON HUMAN NATURE
AND CULTURE

DEREK FREEMAN

Foreword by James J. Fox

PRESS

Published by ANU Press
The Australian National University
Acton ACT 2601, Australia
Email: anupress@anu.edu.au
This title is also available online at press.anu.edu.au

National Library of Australia Cataloguing-in-Publication entry

Creator: Freeman, Derek (John Derek), 1916-2001, author.

Title: Dilthey's dream : essays on human nature and culture / Derek
            Freeman.

ISBN: 9781922144805 (paperback) 9781922144812 (ebook)

Subjects: Anthropology.
            Ethnology.
            Human behavior.
            Nature and nurture.
            Social evolution.

Cover design and layout by ANU Press.

Contents

Foreword

James J. Fox

An Introduction to a Dream

Derek Freeman chose the title *Dilthey's Dream* for this collection of essays and in the first essay of the volume, 'Human Nature and Culture', he explains the significance of this choice of titles. Dilthey's dream offers a vivid metaphor for the fundamental fissure, which had begun to develop in the 19th century, between naturalist and idealist modes of inquiry in the human sciences. Throughout the 20th century, this fissure has become a widening gulf and it was to bridge this gulf that Freeman devoted much of his research career.

In the six elegant essays that comprise this volume, Freeman offers critical arguments for an alternative — 'interactionist' — paradigm for social inquiry. Written at intervals over a period of more than 30 years, these essays — each of which was delivered as a public lecture — mark the progressive articulation of his thinking and his attempt to give an intellectual context to his ideas. The paradigm that he sets forth is intended to constitute a new 'science of human values' firmly grounded in an evolutionary understanding of human nature but recognising individuals' capacities for choice and the consequences of these choices for the adaptive diversity of the human species.

At the time when he began to develop his ideas, Freeman was a lone voice in Australian anthropology arguing for the vigorous engagement of anthropology with the biological sciences. His starting point was a rejection of what he regarded as a dominant 'culturalist' perspective, which he ascribed to Franz Boas's influence on American anthropology. It is important to recognise that the critical first essay in this volume was written in 1969. It contains, in embryo, many of the ideas Freeman was to develop over the next 30 years. There is thus a remarkable intellectual consistency in the critique of Boas's cultural determinism in the first essay of the volume and his historical analysis of the influence of 'Boasian culturalism' in the final essay.

Those readers who are chiefly familiar with Freeman because of the controversy that arose through his criticism of Margaret Mead's research on Samoa may not fully appreciate that, from the outset, Freeman's primary focus was always directed to the ideas of her teacher, Franz Boas. Freeman saw Mead's first youthful monograph, *Coming of Age in Samoa,* as a key text in support of Boas's cultural perspective and his refutation of its claims was the means of undermining such ideas. The essays in this volume thus make clear the intellectual issues that Freeman saw as central to his critical efforts.

An Intellectual Journey from Samoa to Samoa

It was in 1938, while Freeman was a student at Victoria University College in Wellington, that he became acquainted with Mead's research on Samoa. Ernest Beaglehole, who had studied anthropology at Yale University, recommended that Freeman read *Coming of Age in Samoa.* A year later Freeman applied for a position as a teacher in Western Samoa. His intention, as he has described it, was 'to support Mead's already celebrated findings' with research of his own. He was thus, at an early age, an unquestioning supporter of the Boasian traditions of cultural anthropology.

By April 1940, he had arrived in Apia to take up his assignment and he remained on Samoa until November 1943. As a local schoolteacher, Freeman immersed himself in the study of the Samoan language and, after two years, he decided that he had sufficient fluency to undertake more intensive anthropological research. He chose to do research on the local polity of Sa'anapu, a settlement at the time of some 400 inhabitants.

In 1942, in Sa'anapu, Freeman came to know the senior chief, Lauvi Vainu'u, and his youngest son, Fa'imoto. When Fa'imoto died suddenly, Lauvi made Freeman his adopted son and invited him to reside within his house. Later in 1943, the chiefs of Sa'anapu conferred upon him one of their titles, Logona-i-Taga, giving him the right to attend all chiefly assemblies.

Less than a year into his local research on Samoan social life, Freeman decided to leave Sa'anapu to join the New Zealand Volunteer Naval Reserve. Although he visited Samoa briefly in 1946, he did not return to resume his anthropological research in Sa'anapu until 1968.

During the intervening 25 years, Freeman established himself as a notable ethnographer and an important figure in social anthropology. In 1948, on the basis of a thesis, *The Social Structure of a Samoan Village Community,* Freeman was awarded a postgraduate Diploma in Anthropology from the University of London and was then given the opportunity to do fieldwork among the Iban of Sarawak. Between 1951 and 1953, based on this research in Sarawak from January 1949 to June 1951, Freeman produced both a major study, *Report on the Iban,* for the Government of Sarawak and his PhD dissertation, *Family and Kin among the Iban of Sarawak,* for Cambridge University. In July 1954, he was appointed a Senior Fellow in Anthropology in the Research School of Pacific Studies at The Australian National University. He remained in the Department of Anthropology throughout his career.

During the 1950s, Freeman's work was preoccupied with issues of kinship and social organisation. His ethnographic researches on the Iban were exceptional for their detail and their insights. *Report on the Iban* was reprinted in 1970 in the London School of Economics Monographs in Social Anthropology as a modern-day classic in social anthropology.

By the early 1960s, however, Freeman had begun to question the narrow basis of the anthropological methods and theory he had been taught and turned from the study of rules and structures to an exploration of psychoanalysis, ethology and evolutionary biology. He became acquainted with the ideas of Karl Popper with whom he established a long correspondence. Following this change in research directions, Freeman took leave from ANU in 1963 to study at the London Institute of Psychoanalysis. He attended seminars at the Tavistock Clinic given by John Bowlby and travelled to Germany to consult with Konrad Lorenz and I. Eibl-Eibesfeldt about his plans for research in human ethology. During this period. Freeman began to envision the possibilities of a new biologically attuned science of human values.

On the return voyage to Australia in 1964 Freeman re-read, after many years, Margaret Mead's *Coming of Age in Samoa* and, with new awareness, recognised the book's relativist premises and its lack of any biological understanding of adolescent behaviour. He resolved to return to Samoa and resume his own researches from his newfound behavioural and philosophical perspectives.

Two years later, Freeman succeeded in obtaining further leave from the University. With his wife and two daughters, he returned to the village of Sa'anapu and lived there for a full two years, from the beginning of 1966 to the end of 1967. During this period, he purposely visited Manu'a, the main location of Mead's research and began his own inquiries which eventually led to his refutation of Mead's earlier work in Samoa.

In 1968, Freeman returned to Canberra and immediately embarked on developing his views of a new 'interactionist' paradigm. He saw two aspects to this task. The first was to set forth his intellectual vision; the second was to demonstrate the inadequacies of Mead's research on Samoa because it represented for him one of the cornerstones of an anthropological edifice that he rejected. The essays in this volume, the first of which appeared in an ANU publication, *Man and the New Biology*, in 1970, document successive stages in this intellectual journey.

Sailing in Deep Waters: The Mead Controversy

Derek Freeman invariably infused his work with personal intensity and single-minded attention. Ideas were of the utmost importance and his intellectual interests provided compelling guidance for the way he lived. For this reason, once he had become engaged in the controversy over Mead's work after the publication of his book *Margaret Mead and Samoa: The Making and Unmaking of an Anthropological Myth* in 1983, he could, in no way, abandon his position in response to the outcry in support of Margaret Mead. In the words of the Samoan proverb which he enjoyed quoting: 'The qualities of a canoe are tested in deep waters.'

Again and again, in this testing time, he felt compelled to reply to his critics, even the most minor and the least understanding of them. For 20 years in his retirement, he kept up a steady stream of answers to these critics. Each time he returned to the fray, he refined and extended the scope of his arguments. His chief response was to write a sequel, *The Fateful Hoaxing of Margaret Mead,* in 1999, which is a meticulous and engagingly sympathetic account of Mead's time in Samoa based mainly on her own diaries and letters held in the Library of Congress.

Even after this second book had appeared, the controversy persisted and Freeman continued to uncover further evidence in support of his views. The final essay in this volume, written in March 2001 just before his death, is his parting statement on the controversy. He concludes this essay with the words: 'The controversy over Margaret Mead's Samoan fieldwork is then, for me, finally at an end.'

Two qualities are evident in all of Freeman's writings: a felicity of expression and a display of erudition. Freeman had an engaging style of writing and he saw no need to separate poetry from biology in arguing for an anthropology of choice or in writing in praise of heresy. In fashioning his arguments, he was as likely to quote Shakespeare or Auden, as he would Darwin, Huxley or Popper. In his scientific and humanist concerns, he invoked the value of Buddhist heedfulness and, like Huxley, was drawn to the practice of Buddhist ethical precepts.

CHAPTER 1

Human Nature and Culture[1]

Wilhelm Dilthey, the German neo-Kantian philosopher, has left us an account of how, on a night in 1894, there came to him an unnervingly ominous dream. He was staying at a castle in Silesia and, after a long and soul-stirring philosophical discussion, had retired to his bedroom, where there hung a copy of Raphael's famous fresco *The School of Athens*. As Dilthey slept, Raphael's painting came alive as philosophers of post-Renaissance times trooped in to join the ancients and the medievals; whereupon, the whole throng began to separate as though into opposing factions. To one side, around Archimedes and Ptolemy, the naturalistic thinkers gathered; on the other, the idealist philosophers around Socrates and Plato, with bands of mediators forming and re-forming in between. Then, as if impelled by some imperious force, all mediation having failed, the groupings began to recede one from the other, and great fissures opened in the ground between them as they were enveloped in hostile alienation.[2] At this awesome sight, Dilthey was overcome with anxiety; he felt, he tells us, as though the unity of his being was being torn asunder.

I have recounted this dread dream of Dilthey's because it prophetically epitomises what was indeed to happen to the sciences of man during the immediately ensuing decades, and points to consequences from which these sciences still suffer — some of them to the very marrow of their methodologies.

---

1   Reprinted from *Man and the New Biology* (Canberra. Australian National University Press, 1970).

2   W. Kluback, *Wilhelm Dilthey's Philosophy of History* (New York, Columbia University Press, 1956), pp. 103ff; H.A. Hodges, *The Philosophy of Wilhelm Dilthey* (London, Routledge and Kegan Paul, 1952), pp. 312ff.

Charles Darwin, when he came to the end of his essay of 1859, *The Origin of Species by Means of Natural Selection*, appended the laconic words: 'much light will be thrown on the origin of man and his history'.[3] With this aside — surely among the most pregnant in the brief history of science — was opened up the prospect that at least some members of 'Adam's sovereign clone' might transcend the banalities of their creation myth, and by dint of scientific inquiry, eventually come to a more truthful realisation of the realities of their phylogenetic past and of the springs of their evolving human nature.

In recent years, evolutionary theory has emerged saliently as the unifying paradigm of all the biological sciences, from biochemistry to ecology,[4] and its status has been radically enhanced by the advances of the last two decades in molecular biology, which as Muller put it, rank 'among the most magnificent and thrilling of all scientific revolutions that mankind has achieved thus far'.[5] So, with the discovery of the way in which genetic information can be stored on nucleic acid, the molecular basis of the evolutionary process has been revealed, and it has become apparent that 'the great specificity and subtlety shown by any particular enzyme'[6] are as much the result of natural selection as the clinging behaviour of a new-born langur monkey or the capacity of an infant *Homo sapiens* to learn one of the modes of symbolic communication characteristic of his species.[7] Indeed, no informed biologist can now have grounds for disagreement with Muller's generalisation that 'the criterion for any material's having life is whether or not it has the potentiality ... of evolution by Darwinian natural selection'.[8]

Evolutionary theory then, provides a unifying paradigm for all the biological sciences — but it was not always so, and, if we are to grasp the significance of the new biology for the understanding of man and

---

3   C. Darwin, *The Origin of Species by Means of Natural Selection* (London, John Murray, 1859), p. 488.

4   E. Mayr, *Animal Species and Evolution* (Cambridge. Mass., Harvard University Press, 1963), p. 1.

5   H.J. Muller, 'Means and aims of human genetic betterment', in *The Control of Human Heredity and Evolution*, ed. T.M. Sonneborn (New York, Macmillan. 1965), p. 101.

6   F. Crick, *Of Molecules and Men* (Seattle and London, University of Washington Press, 1966). p. 52.

7   P. Jay, 'Mother–infant relations in langurs', in *Maternal Behaviour in Mammals*, ed. H. Rheingold (New York. John Wiley 1963), p. 286; E.H. Lenneberg, *Biological Foundations of Language* (New York, John Wiley, 1967), p. 28 and pp. 128ff.

8   Muller, 'The gene material as the initiator and the organizing basis of life', in *Heritage from Mendel*, ed. R.A. Brink (Madison, University of Wisconsin Press, 1967), p. 443.

his behaviour, we must — paradoxically — return to the 19th century and relate the symbolism of Dilthey's dream to the vicissitudes of Darwin's theory.

The intellectual commotion that followed the publication of the *Origin of Species* is well enough known.[9] A comparable furore was created by the appearance, in 1871, of *The Descent of Man*.[10] As Tylor noted, during that same year, to many there seemed 'something presumptuous and repulsive' in the view that the history of mankind was 'part and parcel of the history of nature',[11] and so, during the last decades of the 19th century, there arose a number of related ideologies opposed to the notion of a naturalistic and evolutionary science of man. Moreover, not a few of those involved were themselves men of science. For example, it was Rudolf Virchow, celebrated for his contributions to cellular pathology, who at Munich in 1877 vehemently attacked Haeckel's 'monistic view of the origin and nature of man'.[12] Indeed, so deeply felt was Virchow's opposition that he gave voice to fears that 'the theory of descent' might bring to Germany the horrors of the Paris Commune, and then proceeded, on the basis of his own researches in 'the domain of prehistoric anthropology', vigorously to contest the theory that man was phylogenetically 'allied to the rest of the animal world'.[13]

While Virchow was thus combating 'the incubus called Descent',[14] a young man named Franz Boas, who was to become the founder and father of cultural anthropology in America, had already begun his studies in the physical sciences at Kiel. A few years later, in Berlin, the young Dr Boas came profoundly under the influence both of Virchow (with whom he came to share a life-long antipathy to evolutionary biology), and of neo-Kantian idealism, which led him to abandon the mechanistic

---

9   G. de Beer, *Charles Darwin: Evolution by Natural Selection* (London, Nelson, 1963), chapter 8.

10   F. Darwin (ed.), *The Life and Letters of Charles Darwin* (London, John Murray, 1888), Vol. III, p. 133.

11   E.B. Tylor, *Primitive Culture* (London, John Murray, 1871). p. 2.

12   E. Haeckel, 'Charles Darwin as an anthropologist', in *Darwin and Modern Science*, ed. A.C. Seward (Cambridge, University Press, 1909), p. 145; cf. also *Nature* (1877), 16:491.

13   R. Virchow, 'The liberty of science in the modern state', *Nature* (1877), 17:74 and 112.

14   This was the phrase of Adolf Bastian, friend and collaborator of Rudolf Virchow, who was also an inveterate opponent of evolutionary theory; cf. Haeckel, *Freedom in Science and Teaching* (London, Kegan Paul, 1879), p. 7.

Weltanschauung of the natural sciences.[15] In 1885 he was to take these beliefs with him to America, and, in 1894 — the year of Dilthey's dream — in an address to the American Association for the Advancement of Science,[16] Boas propounded the doctrine of cultural determinism, which as it became adopted by his students was to culminate in the alienation of cultural anthropology from the biological sciences in general, and from evolutionary biology in particular.

And that same year, in Europe, Emile Durkheim (an exact contemporary of Boas) was preparing for publication his treatise *Les règles de la méthode sociologique* which propounded the doctrine that 'social facts' were entirely unrelated to biological facts,[17] and so opened up a methodological chasm between sociology and the biological study of human societies.

So it was, with the doctrines of Boas and Durkheim as the catalysts of fission, that the social sciences began to recede from the biological and natural sciences. Dilthey's dream was being methodically acted out, and the stage was being set for the sterile nature–nurture controversies of the 1920s — of which we are all the intellectual heirs.

The most eminent of Boas's early students was Alfred Kroeber, who likewise evinced a keen antipathy to evolutionary theory, and was apt, at this period, to refer to those 'infected with biological methods of thought'.[18] Characteristically, it was Kroeber, in a series of papers beginning in 1915, who pursued to its methodological extreme the doctrine of cultural determinism he had acquired from Boas, arguing, with emphatic rhetoric, that there was an 'eternal chasm' between the cultural and biological. There was, proclaimed Kroeber (and his language could not have been more sweeping), an 'utter divergence between social and organic forces'; culture was 'an entity in itself', and entirely unconnected with the biological order and evolutionary process.[19] With this doctrine went a series of rudimentary assumptions which soon became fundamental to anthropological

---

15   C. Kluckhohn and O. Prufer, 'Influences during the formative years', in *The Anthropology of Franz Boas*, ed. W. Goldschmidt (American Anthropological Association, Memoir No. 89, 1959), pp. 9ff; P. Radin, 'The mind of primitive man', *New Republic* (1939), 98:303; G. Stocking, *Race, Culture and Evolution* (New York, Free Press, 1968), p. 138.

16   F. Boas, 'Human faculty as determined by race', *Proceedings, American Association for the Advancement of Science* (1894), 43:218.

17   E. Durkheim, *Les règles de la méthode sociologique* (Paris, 1895).

18   A.L. Kroeber, 'Inheritance by magic', *American Anthropologist* (1916), 18:34.

19   Kroeber, 'Eighteen professions', *American Anthropologist* (1915), 17:283–288; 'The superorganic', ibid. (1917), 19:163–213.

orthodoxy: human nature was (as Margaret Mead was subsequently to put it) 'the rawest, most undifferentiated of raw material';[20] there was, it was held, a 'generic unity' or 'equivalence of hereditary endowment' throughout the entire human species;[21] and from these two assumptions a third was derived, the conclusion that 'every human expression' was completely moulded by 'social conditioning'.[22] Biological variables, by arbitrary pronouncement, had been completely excluded.

These implacable departures in cultural anthropology were paralleled by a militant movement in psychology, begun in about 1913 by John B. Watson, which came to be known as Behaviourism.[23] Initially, Watson was concerned primarily with breaking free from introspectionism, and he wrote bravely of his vision of psychology as 'a purely objective experimental branch of natural science'.[24] In the early 1920s, however, with Watson's resignation from Johns Hopkins University to become (in 1924) an advertising executive,[25] and under the influence of the anti-instinct movement in American social psychology,[26] Behaviourism became transformed into a rhetorical crusade against the recognition of biologically determined variables in human behaviour. Within a few years, Watson was declaiming to the world that there was 'no such thing as any inheritance of capacity, talent, temperament, mental constitution and characteristics', and that 'nurture not nature' was responsible for what a child became in life.[27]

The distinction between nature and nurture is a hoary one; Prospero, it will be recollected, described the abhorred Caliban as 'a devil, a born devil, on whose nature, nurture can never stick'.[28] In the 1870s these terms were brought into scientific discourse by Galton in his pioneer researches

20   M. Mead, 'Growing up in New Guinea' (1930), in *From the South Seas* (New York, Morrow, 1939), p. 212.

21   Boas, *The Mind of Primitive Man* (New York, Macmillan, 1911), p. 155; L. Spier, 'Franz Boas and some of his views', *Acta Americana* (1943), 1:108.

22   Spier, 'Some central elements in the legacy', in *The Anthropology of Franz Boas*, p. 146.

23   J.C. Burnham, 'On the origins of behaviorism', *Journal of the History of the Behavioral Sciences* (1968), 4:143–151.

24   J.B. Watson, 'Psychology as the behaviorist views it', *Psychological Review* (1913), 20:158.

25   Watson in *A History of Psychology in Autobiography*, ed. C. Murchison (Worcester, Mass. Clark University Press, 1936), Vol. 3, pp. 279ff.

26   G. Adams. 'Human Instincts', *American Mercury* (1928), 14:458.

27   Watson, *Behaviorism* (New York, Norton and Co., 1925), p. 74; 'What is behaviorism?' *Harper's Magazine* (1926), 152:729.

28   W. Shakespeare, *The Tempest*, Act IV, Scene 1.

on the life histories of identical twins.[29] However, at least since the time of Johannsen's fundamental distinction (of 1909) between genotype and phenotype,[30] no informed biologist has opposed heredity to environment as though the one might be wholly dominant over the other. Indeed, as Zirkle has pointed out, 'any attempt to make one more important than the other is as silly as trying to determine which is the more important in deriving a product, the multiplicand or the multiplier'.[31] In other words, on the nature–nurture issue biologists have long taken an interactionist position. As Dobzhansky has recently phrased it: 'The genotype and the environment are equally important, because both are indispensable. There is no organism without genes, and any genotype can only act in some environment.'[32] So, in 1915, while Kroeber was professing that 'heredity cannot be allowed to have acted any part in history',[33] we find the biologist Conklin (in the first edition of his book *Heredity and Environment in the Development of Man*) declaring that 'neither environment nor heredity is all-important ... both are necessary to development'.[34]

At this distance in time it is a matter for wonderment that Kroeber, Watson and the other fervent environmentalists of the 1920s should have had the intellectual temerity to take the extreme stance that they did. Their behaviour becomes understandable, however, when it is realised that biology, during the first quarter of this century, was itself in a state of profound confusion.

In 1880, in celebrating the 'coming of age' of *The Origin of Species*, in a lecture at the Royal Institution, T.H. Huxley felt justified in declaring that Evolution had taken its place 'alongside of those accepted truths which must be taken into account by philosophers of all schools'.[35] Within a few years of Darwin's death in 1882, however, the situation had begun to change. First came Weismann's trenchant critique of the doctrine of

---

29   F. Galton, 'The history of twins as a criterion of the relative powers of nature and nurture', *Journal of the Anthropological Institute* (1875), 5:391–406.

30   W. Johannsen, *Elemente der exakten Erblichkeit* (Jena, Fischer, 1909).

31   C. Zirkle, *Evolution, Marxian Biology and the Social Scene* (Philadelphia, University of Pennsylvania Press, 1959), p. 447.

32   T. Dobzhansky, *Heredity and the Nature of Man* (New York, Harcourt, Brace and World, 1964), p. 55.

33   Kroeber, 'Eighteen professions', *American Anthropologist* (1915), 17:285.

34   E.G. Conklin, *Heredity and Environment in the Development of Man*, rev. ed. (Princeton, University Press, 1930), p. 72. (First edition was in February 1915.)

35   T.H. Huxley, 'The coming of age of the Origin of Species', *Nature* (1880), 22:4.

the inheritance of acquired characters,[36] a doctrine which Darwin himself had incorporated into evolutionary theory in the shape of his sterile Pangenesis hypothesis of 1868.[37] From the 1890s onward, other biologists began to express discontent with the principle of natural selection. With the unearthing, in 1900, of Mendel's results, a vain quarrel began between the mutationists and biometricians,[38] with the mutationists expressing ever-increasing doubts as to the efficacy of natural selection, until, in April 1914, we find Karl Pearson lamenting that the work of Darwin was being 'largely undermined'.[39] Later that same year — in Australia — in his Presidential Address to the British Association,[40] William Bateson conclusively rejected Darwinian theory, and, falling back on preformist notions, advanced the view that all cases of genetic variation might be due to the loss of elements present in an original complex. Bateson's views were widely publicised,[41] and were greeted sympathetically by the leading American geneticist T.H. Morgan, who, at that time, also held a mutationist theory of evolution.[42] Soon after this, Jennings was telling the Washington Academy of Sciences that 'the evolutionists might almost feel that the enemy had crept into their citadel and was blowing it up from within';[43] and, by 1922, in the course of a British Association symposium

---

36   Weismann's criticism of the doctrine of acquired characters was initiated by his remarks on heredity and the 'continuity of the germ-plasm' at a meeting held on 21 June 1883, when he was tendered the position of Vice-Rector of the University of Freiburg; cf. L. Cuénot, 'The inheritance of acquired characters', *Annual Report, Smithsonian Institution* (for the year ending 30 June 1921) (Washington, Government Printing Office, 1922), p. 336; cf. also A. Weismann, *The Germ-plasm: a Theory of Heredity* (London, Walter Scott, 1893).

37   C. Darwin, *Variation of Animals and Plants under Domestication* (London, John Murray, 1868), Vol. 2, chapter xxvii.

38   R.C. Punnett, 'The early days of genetics', *Heredity* (1950), 4:1–10, G.S. Carter, *A Hundred Years of Evolution* (London, Sidgwick and Jackson), p. 121; Mayr, 'Where are we?', *Cold Spring Harbor Symposia on Quantitative Biology* (1959), 24:1ff.

39   K. Pearson, *The Life, Letters and Labours of Francis Galton* (Cambridge, University Press, 1914), Vol. 1, p. vi: in preface dated Gallon Laboratory, 8 April 1914.

40   As President of the Eighty-Fourth Meeting of the British Association for the Advancement of Science, William Bateson delivered two addresses, the first in Melbourne on 14 August 1914 and the second in Sydney on 20 August 1914; cf. *Report of the Eighty-Fourth Meeting of the British Association for the Advancement of Science, Australia, 1914* (London, John Murray, 1915), pp. 3–38.

41   William Bateson's presidential addresses were also published in *Nature* (93:635–642, 674–681), *Science* (40:287–302, 319–333), and in the *Annual Report (for 1915) of the Smithsonian Institution* (Washington, Government Printing Office, 1916), pp. 359–394.

42   T.H. Morgan, *A Critique of the Theory of Evolution* (Princeton, Princeton University Press, 1916); cf. also E.G. Jeffrey, 'Drosophila and the mutation hypothesis', *Science* (1925), 62:3–5.

43   H.S. Jennings, 'Observed changes in hereditary characters in relation to evolution', *Journal of the Washington Academy of Sciences* (1917), 7:283.

on Darwinism, as part of a chorus of criticism by Willis[44] and other eminent biologists, J.T. Cunningham was giving it as his opinion that natural selection was 'as extinct as the dodo'.[45]

By this time Fisher and Haldane[46] had already begun the mathematical researches, which, with those of Sewall Wright and others,[47] were to reconcile the facts of genetics with the process of natural selection, and to result in the rise of the synthetic theory of evolution — that 'mutated phoenix' (as Julian Huxley has called it)[48] — which now reigns supreme in modern biology. But this new epoch did not effectively begin until about 1930, with the publication of Fisher's classic essay *The Genetical Theory of Natural Selection,* and, during most of the second and third decades of this century, evolutionary biology was beset by discord and confusion.[49]

So it was that during this period, Kroeber, Watson and others were able to promulgate their extreme environmentalist views. Behaviourism, it is instructive to note, was based on 'tacit assumptions' almost identical with those of cultural anthropology, these assumptions being, as the Brelands

---

44   J.C. Willis, 'The inadequacy of the theory of natural selection as an explanation of the facts of geographical distribution and evolution', *Report of the Ninetieth Meeting of the British Association for the Advancement of Science,* Hull, 1922 (London, John Murray, 1923), p. 399; cf. also Willis, *Age and Area* (Cambridge, University Press, 1922).

45   Cf. *Nature* (1922), 110:752; J.R. Cunningham was one of the participants in a symposium on 'The Present Position of Darwinism', held jointly by the botanical and zoological sections during the course of the Ninetieth Meeting of the British Association for the Advancement of Science at Hull in September 1922. In his presidential address to Section K (Botany) at the Eighty-Ninth Meeting of the British Association in Edinburgh on 9 September 1921, Professor D.H. Scott, F.R.S., had given it as his opinion that 'for the moment, at all events, the Darwinian period is past' (cf. *Nature* (1921), 108:154); and later that year in Toronto, on 28 December 1921, William Bateson, in an address to the American Association for the Advancement of Science, renewed his criticism of the Darwinian theory of evolution by natural selection (cf. *Science* (1922), 55:55–61). Bateson's views were given great notice in the popular press, (cf. H.F. Osborn, 'William Bateson on Darwinism', *Science* (1922), 53:194–197), and were used by those who in the immediately following years attempted to suppress the teaching of evolutionary theory in certain of the southern and western states of the USA (cf. W. Bateson, 'The revolt against the teaching of evolution in the United States', *Nature* (1923), 112:313–314; including Bateson's statement that it was he who 'all unwittingly dropped the spark which started the fire').

46   R.A. Fisher, 'The correlations between relatives on the supposition of Mendelian inheritance', *Transactions, Royal Society of Edinburgh* (1918), 52:399–433; cf. also J.B.S. Haldane's papers on 'A mathematical theory of natural and artificial selection', which were published in the *Proceedings of the Cambridge Philosophical Society* from 1924 onwards, and which were summarised in Haldane's *The Causes of Evolution* (London, Longmans Green, 1932), pp. 171–215.

47   S. Wright, 'Evolution in Mendelian populations', *Genetics* (1931), 16:97–159; cf. also Wright, *Evolution and the Genetics of Populations,* Vol. 1, *Genetic and biometric foundations* (Chicago and London, University of Chicago Press, 1968); A.H. Sturtevant, *A History of Genetics* (New York, Harper and Row, 1965), chapter 17.

48   Julian Huxley, *Evolution: The Modern Synthesis* (London, George Allen and Unwin, 1942), p. 28.

49   de Beer, *Charles Darwin: Evolution by Natural Selection,* p. 183.

have stated them, that 'the animal comes to the laboratory as a virtual *tabula rasa,* that species differences are insignificant, and that all responses are about equally conditionable to all stimuli'.[50] Here also, it will be observed, phylogenetically given variables are arbitrarily excluded.

Whatever may have been the scientific inadequacies of Behaviourism, its appeal was immense. Watson's book of popular lectures, when it was first published in 1925, was declared in the *New York Herald-Tribune* to be perhaps the 'most important book ever written',[51] and his doctrines soon became the gospel of the late 1920s. By 1927, V.F. Calverton, in the *Modern Quarterly,*[52] was referring to environmentalism as the 'great movement' underlying contemporary thought, and there was talk of 'a new enlightenment'.[53] The analysis of this fascinating epoch in intellectual history I must leave to another occasion. For the present, I only wish to note that the paradigm in terms of which many of the social sciences still operate was largely derived from the doctrines and assumptions of the uncompromising environmentalism of the 1920s and 1930s. Moreover, it is in the murky light of this paradigm that many educated people still think about human nature and culture. What bearing, then, have the advances of the last few decades in the biological sciences had on the doctrines and assumptions of such men as Kroeber and Watson, and on the related paradigm of certain of the social sciences?

Let me begin with an examination of the assumption that in all human populations there is an 'equivalence of hereditary endowment'. This assumption, often also referred to as the principle of the psychic unity of mankind,[54] is akin to the widespread notion that there is a unitary and uniform nature which we all share, and which, one of these days when we have sufficient knowledge, it will be possible to typify. We are here confronted with an example of typological thinking of a kind that is quite incompatible with the findings of modern population genetics. In Ernst Mayr's judgment, 'the replacement of typological thinking by population thinking is perhaps the greatest conceptual revolution that has taken place in biology';[55] without question, it is an innovation in understanding that is fundamental to the new biology.

---

50   K. and M. Breland, 'The misbehavior of organisms', in *Readings in Animal Behavior*, ed. T.E. McGill (New York, Holt, Rinehart and Winston, 1965), p. 459.

51   Cf. *Nation*, 13 January 1926.

52   V.F. Calverton, 'The analysis of behavior', *Modern Quarterly* (1927), 4:302.

53   S.D. Schmalhausen, *Why We Misbehave* (New York, Macauley, 1928), p. 17.

54   M. Harris, *The Rise of Anthropological Theory* (London, Routledge and Kegan Paul, 1968), p. 15.

55   Mayr, *Animal Species and Evolution*, p. 5.

With the recognition of the fact that the genetic processes involved in evolution operate in populations, there has, in recent decades, been much research in this field, and one of the notable outcomes has been the demonstration that natural populations of outbreeding diploid species, including man, far from being genetically uniform, are genetically highly heterogeneous.[56] Furthermore, this genetic diversity is seen as adaptive, for in many vertebrate species it is an array of genotypes which enables a Mendelian population both to maintain its hold on any particular ecological niche, and to react adaptively to environmental change. This diverse array of genotypes within an outbreeding population is due to the independent behaviour of chromosome pairs during meiosis. Thus man, with 23 chromosome pairs, produces gametes (or germ cells) with any of the two to the power 23 alternative genomes (or haploid chromosome sets). This, as Hirsch has pointed out, makes 'vanishingly small' the chance that any two children of a given sexual union (with the exception, of course, of monozygotic twins) will be genetically identical, the probability as Hirsch has calculated it) being less than 1 in over 70 trillion.[57] The probability that two unrelated individuals will have the same genotype is effectively nil. In other words, all human beings (with the exception, again, of monozygotes), from the time of their conception, possess a genotype or biological endowment of a *uniquely individual kind*. It follows, as Dobzhansky has phrased it, that 'the nature of man as a species resolves itself into a great multitude of human natures', and that human nature is 'not unitary but multiform'.[58]

---

56   J.M. Thoday, 'Selection and genetic heterogeneity', in *Genetic Diversity and Human Behavior*, ed. J.N. Spuhler (Chicago, Aldine Publishing Co., 1967), pp. 89–98.

57   J. Hirsch, 'Behavior genetics and individuality understood', *Science* (1963), 142:1437. It should be noted that the trillion is here the American one (10^{12}). As Professor D.G. Catcheside, F.R.S. (Director, Research School of Biological Sciences, The Australian National University) has kindly pointed out to me, the situation is, in fact, not so simple as '2^{23} alternative genomes', where the assumption is made that each of these is different, which is further dependent on the assumption that the two members of each chromosome pair are different. Professor Catcheside comments: 'While this is probable in man and other outbreeding organisms, it is not necessarily true. However, the diversity is likely to be increased by virtue of any pairs of chromosomes within which there are two or more genetic differences which may be reassorted by crossing over. Thus the possible number of gametes is decreased by a factor of two for every chromosome pair which has no genetic difference between its members and increased by a factor of two for each genetic difference in excess of one in each chromosome pair with two or more differences'.

58   Dobzhansky, *Heredity and the Nature of Man*, p.49: 'Of flies and man', *American Psychologist* (1967), 22:42.

This is not, of course, to deny that there are behavioural mechanisms specific to all members of the human species; what it does mean is that due regard must be paid to individual variability in any comparative study of these mechanisms. Further, there are now sound scientific grounds for the full recognition of individuality in the analysis of social and cultural behaviour; the way in which one individual plays a role (however it be ritualised) will be different from the way the next individual plays it, and this difference, the evidence indicates, will, to a significant degree, be genetically determined.

It also follows from the discoveries of population genetics that a human being, when he issues from his mother's womb, is not, in behavioural terms, a *tabula rasa,* and the 'most undifferentiated of raw material', for, as we have seen, human beings are intrinsically variable before they undergo differentiating experiences.[59] This conclusion, moreover, has been borne out in recent years by researches carried out at the Neonatal Behavioural Laboratory at the Albert Einstein College of Medicine, which have demonstrated 'consistent individual differences in response intensity' in human neonates 'during the first few days of life'.[60]

The notion, so prevalent among psychologists and anthropologists in the 1920s and 1930s, that the human neonate was a mere 'reaction-machine',[61] was accompanied, as might be expected, by a total rejection of evolutionary theory, or 'the mentalistic continuity doctrine', as a prominent psychologist of the time scathingly called it.[62] Thus, the view that man's behavioural repertoire might, in significant ways, be phylogenetically determined was completely rejected, and it was held, as the social psychologist Kantor stated it in 1924, that for the human species, behaviour began and ended with 'the individual's actual interactions with his stimuli conditions'.[63]

This simple-minded, stimulus-response, chain-reflex model of behaviour was essentially a speculative construct owing nothing to the findings of comparative neurophysiology as they then existed, for it was at this

---

59   Hirsch, 'Behavior genetics and individuality understood', p. 1437.
60   W.H. Bridger and B. Birns, 'Experience and temperament in human neonates', in *Early Experience and Behaviour: The psychobiology of development,* ed. G. Newton and S. Levine (Springfield, Illinois, Charles C. Thomas, 1968), p. 89; cf. also H. Papousek, 'Genetics and child development', in *Genetic Diversity and Human Behavior,* pp. 171–186.
61   Calverton, 'The rise of objective psychology', *Psychological Review* (1924), 31:426.
62   J.R. Kantor, 'An attempt toward a naturalistic description of emotions', *Psychological Review* (1921), 28:131.
63   Kantor, *Principles of Psychology* (New York, Knopf, 1924), p. 172.

very time that the meticulous experimental research of men like Coghill and Lashley[64] was demonstrating conclusively the scientific inadequacy of an empty-organism, peripheralist paradigm. Soon after this, von Holst disproved the chain-reflex hypothesis[65] by demonstrating, for example, that a completely deafferented spinal eel can still swim in a well co-ordinated manner. And this was followed by the brilliantly executed researches of Weiss and many others[66] in which the neuro-muscular connections in various vertebrates were surgically rearranged. In no instance could the animals operated on learn to overcome the anatomical disarrangement. These and other comparable experiments showed, in the words of Lenneberg, 'that motor co-ordination (and certain behaviour patterns dependent upon it) is driven by a rigid, unalterable cycle of neuro-physiological events inherent in a species' central nervous system'.[67] This conclusion that certain of the basic behaviour mechanisms of a species are phylogenetically programmed in the central nervous and related systems was further demonstrated, from the 1950s onwards, by the researches of such notable investigators as von Holst, MacLean, Delgado, Penfield and Heath,[68] in which the brains of a variety of vertebrate species, including man, were explored by the method of direct electrical stimulation by means of implanted micro-electrodes.

---

64 G.E. Coghill, *Anatomy and the Problem of Behavior* (New York, Macmillan, 1929); K.E. Lashley, 'The relation between cerebral mass, learning and retention', *Journal of Comparative Neurology* (1926), 41:1–58.

65 E. von Holst, 'Uber den Prozess der zentralnervösen Koordination', *Pflügers Arch. ges. Physiol.* (1935), 236:149–159; cf. K. Lorenz, 'Morphology and behavior patterns in closely allied species', in *Group Processes, Transactions of the first Conference*, ed. B. Schaffner (New York, Josiah Macy Jr Foundation, 1955), p. 183: 'I think we can now accept it as a fact that the central nervous system can generate and co-ordinate nervous impulses, without any afferent inflow'.

66 P.A. Weiss, 'Experimental analysis of co-ordination by the disarrangement of central–peripheral relations', *Physiological Mechanisms in Animal Behavior: Symposia of the Society for Experimental Biology* (New York, Academic Press, 1950), 4:92–111; cf. also R.W. Sperry, 'Physiological plasticity and brain circuit theory', in *Biological and Biochemical Bases of Behavior*, ed. H.F Harlow and C.N. Woolsey (Madison, University of Wisconsin Press, 1958), pp. 401–424.

67 Lenneberg, *Biological Foundations of Language*, p. 19.

68 E. von Holst and U. von Saint Paul, 'On the functional organization of drives', *Animal Behaviour* (1963), 11:1–20; P.D. MacLean, 'New findings relevant to the evolution of psychosexual functions of the brain', *Journal of Nervous and Mental Disease* (1962), 135:289–301; J.M.R. Delgado, 'Cerebral heterostimulation in a monkey colony', *Science* (1963), 141:1613; W. Penfield and T. Rasmussen, *The Cerebral Cortex of Man: A clinical study of localization of function* (New York, Macmillan, 1952); R.G. Heath, 'Pleasure response of human subjects to direct stimulation of the brain: Physiologic and psychodynamic considerations', in *The Role of Pleasure in Behavior*, ed. R.G. Heath (New York, Hoeber Medical Division, 1964), pp. 219–243.

Much of this work has been undertaken in close conjunction with research by ethologists — whose discoveries and theories are also very much a part of the new biology. The principal achievement of ethology has been the demonstration of the truth of Darwin's supposition (in his book *The Expression of the Emotions in Man and Animals*) that many behaviour mechanisms are phylogenetic adaptations; in other words, that such behaviour mechanisms have evolved in the same manner as other features of animal populations by process of natural selection, and so are transmitted, from generation to generation, in the genetic code. That this in fact occurs in infra-human animals can now, in the light of the findings of ethology and behaviour genetics, be taken as demonstrated.

Indeed, as the behaviour geneticist Aubrey Manning has described,[69] an animal may possess within its nervous system the equivalent of an encoded 'picture' of the normal environment, and the appropriate responses to make to it. Further, the results of a recent experiment by Sackett[70] indicate that comparable innate recognition mechanisms exist even among species of the zoological order to which we ourselves belong. In Sackett's experiment, solitary young rhesus monkeys, reared in isolation from birth, and deprived of any opportunity of observing their own reflections, were enabled, by pressing levers, to project coloured slides on the walls of their cubicles. These slides depicted a range of objects, including a number of monkeys. Sackett's experimental subjects showed a marked preference for pictures of conspecifics, and especially for those of infant rhesus monkeys. Further, an early preference for pictures of threatening older rhesus monkeys persisted until about 2½ months of age, when fear responses were displayed and such pictures were avoided. In view of the fact that these infant monkeys had not experienced any social communication with conspecifics (or any other animal species), their recognition of an expression of threat becomes strong evidence for the existence in the rhesus monkey of phylogenetically programmed receptor mechanisms which make such reception possible.

In infra-human animals, then, the neonate is no behavioural *tabula rasa*. But this fact will cause no surprise to the evolutionary biologist, who recognises how vital to survival certain behaviour mechanisms are;

---

69   A. Manning, 'Drosophila and the evolution of behaviour', in *Viewpoints in Biology*, ed. J.D. Carthy and C.L. Duddington (London, Butterworths, 1965), 4:126.

70   G.R. Sackett, 'Monkeys reared in isolation with pictures as visual input: evidence for an innate releasing mechanism', *Science* (1966), 154:1468–1473; cf. also R.L Fantz, 'The origin of form perception', *Scientific American* (1961), 204(5):66–72.

who understands that these behaviour mechanisms have emerged in the course of evolutionary history because they contributed decisively to the reproductive success of the animal populations in which they were found, and who, from his knowledge of molecular biology, is aware that the genetic code is capable of storing and transmitting a quantum of exceedingly intricate information. As Francis Crick has graphically put it, the DNA molecules from just one sperm cell carry sufficient information, if it were written out, to 'fill about five hundred large books, all different — a fair-sized private library'.[71] An embryo's genotype, then, is an evolved compilation of astonishingly intricate instructions, not only for the building of such a marvellously complex structure as the central nervous system, but also for its behavioural operation. Or, to put it in another way, a genotype is the conditioning with which a living organism enters its environment, fitted to utilise it, this conditioning being the cumulative product of genetic adaptation to a succession of ever-changing environments during countless past generations. And these are conclusions which indubitably apply to us all, for one of the facts of which we may all be sure is that all of our lineal ancestors — back to the Miocene and beyond — reached reproductive age.

What then of the human neonate? Like other primate neonates, we find him equipped with a range of fixed action patterns, such as reflexive rooting and sucking, as well as displaying spontaneous cyclic activity, which as Teitelbaum has remarked,[72] is 'instinctive rather than reflexive', being strongly influenced not merely by external stimuli but by internal states as well. Nonetheless, the manifest behavioural repertoire of a newborn human infant is conspicuously limited. It was this superficial impression, perhaps more than anything else, which led Watson to the facile and erroneous conclusion that in the human species heredity counted for 'almost nothing', and led him to describe the human neonate as 'a piece of unformed protoplasm'.[73] What he failed to realise was that the genetic determination of the behaviour of an individual is far from over at birth. And here we come to the notable discoveries, in recent decades, of developmental biology. In the words of Frank Beach, 'the genotype is in continuous operation as far as its effects on behaviour

---

71 Crick, *Of Molecules and Men*, p. 58.

72 P. Teitelbaum, 'The biology of drive' in *The Neurosciences*, ed. G.C. Quarton, T. Melnechuk and F.O. Schmitt (New York, Rockefeller University Press, 1967), p. 559.

73 J.R. Watson, *Psychological Care of Infant and Child* (London, George Allen and Unwin, 1928), p. 18; Watson et al., 'Is man a machine?' *Forum* (1929), 82:265.

are concerned';[74] and further, it is now known that genes are 'turned on and off' in the course of ontogeny in intimate interaction with the environment, so producing the phenomenon of the critical or sensitive period of behavioural development.

Perhaps the best-known example of this is imprinting in certain species of birds, to which attention was first drawn by Konrad Lorenz in the 1930s.[75] Since then, critical periods for learning have been discovered in a wide range of social animals; among most breeds of dog, for example, as Scott and Fuller report, the optimum period for social bonding is between the sixth and eighth weeks.[76] Similarly, there is now a convincing body of evidence that there is a critical period for primary social bonding in the human species, beginning at a point in maturation reached at about three months or thereabouts, and marked by the onset of a persistent alpha rhythm of three to four waves per second in the electrical activity of the infant's brain.[77] This evidence, moreover, indicates (as does the comparative evidence from primatology)[78] that human kinship behaviour is phylogenetically based — a conclusion with profound implications for social anthropology and allied disciplines. There are also immediately practical implications; for example, J.P. Scott, a distinguished investigator of the process of primary socialisation, counsels those who would acquire a dog to do so, if possible, when it is between six and eight weeks of age; and he has recently advised that the adoption of a human infant should, ideally, occur 'as soon as possible after birth and no later than the first six months of life'.[79]

74   F.A. Beach, 'Ontogeny and living systems', in *Group Processes*, p. 14.
75   K. Lorenz, 'Companionship in bird life' (1935), reprinted in *Instinctive Behavior*, ed, C.H. Schiller (London, Methuen, 1957), pp. 83–128.
76   J.P. Scott and J.L. Fuller, *Genetics and the Social Behavior of the Dog* (Chicago and London, Chicago University Press, 1965), chapter 4.
77   J.P. Scott, 'The process of primary socialization in canine and human infants', *Monograph of the Society for the Research into Child Development* (1963), 28:1–47; D.B. Lindsley in *Brain Function*, ed. C.D. Clernente and D.B. Lindsley (Berkeley and Los Angeles, University of California Press, 1963), 5:73ff.
78   M. Yamada, 'A study of the blood-relationship in the natural society of the Japanese macaque', *Primates* (1963), 4:43–65; A. Tsumori, 'Newly acquired behavior in social interactions of Japanese monkeys', *Social Communication among Primates*, ed. S.A. Altman (Chicago and London, University of Chicago Press, 1967), pp. 207–219; J. van Lawick-Goodall, 'The behaviour of free-living chimpanzees in the Gombe stream reserve', *Animal Behaviour Monographs* (1968), Vol. 1, Part 3, pp. 222ff.
79   Scott, 'The process of primary socialization in the dog', p. 435.

Another instance is the critical period for language acquisition in the human species, the evidence for which has recently been presented by Lenneberg in his book *Biological Foundations of Language*. With the human infant the development of language does not begin until the age of 18 months or thereabouts, at which stage highly complex verbal behaviour is acquired naturally — that is, without formal instruction. We tend to take this extraordinary event, like so many biological phenomena, for granted; but we might well ask why the development of language behaviour does not take place earlier, as at six months when the infant is equally exposed to the verbal behaviour of those around him. The reason, the biological evidence suggests, is because the genetically monitored maturation of the nervous system has not yet reached the requisite sensitive period. When it does, however, the development of verbal behaviour is, as Hockett has expressed it,[80] 'as inevitable as menarche or the appearance of axillary hair, and genetically more stable than either'. In other words, as Lenneberg concludes, 'the processes by which the realized outer structure of a natural language comes about are deeply-rooted species-specific, innate properties of man's biological nature'.[81]

Rousseau in his enchanted dream was convinced that it might be possible to teach apes to converse like men. This, we now know, is 'against the use of nature', for a series of scientific investigations have shown that 'even amid human surroundings' a young chimpanzee 'never prattles and babbles' as a human infant does when beginning to talk,[82] this being for the good reason that the chimpanzee species has not evolved a genotype that permits the development of the brain mechanisms to sustain symbolic verbal behaviour. In such ways, then, whatever be the vaunting whims of men, 'nature her custom holds'.

In discussing the activation of genes during the course of ontogeny I noted that this occurs 'in intimate interaction with the environment'. Let me further emphasise that the recognition of the genetic determinants of behaviour in no wise involves neglect of the environmental determinants. Indeed, one of the major facets of the new biology is the meticulous experimental study of the both profound and subtle ways in which environmental forces influence the development of individual organisms,

---

80   C.F. Hockett, review of *Biological Foundations of Language* by E.H. Lenneberg, *Scientific American* (1967), 217(5):142.
81   Lenneberg, *Biological Foundations of Language*, p. 394.
82   W.N. Kellog, 'Communication and language in home-raised chimpanzees, *Science* (1968), 162:423–426.

and particularly during the course of early experience. It is this which René Dubos has recently called 'Biological Freudianism',[83] and many examples of such research could be cited, from Thompson's experiments on the influence of prenatal maternal anxiety on emotionality in young rats, to Gottlieb's recent demonstration that duck embryos (that is, still in the egg) are influenced by duck noises occurring in the outside world, and that such stimulation is essential to the development of their species-specific auditory perception.[84]

We are here dealing with behavioural plasticity, which is generally characteristic of the most recently evolved vertebrate class, the mammals, and especially characteristic of the most recently evolved order of that class, the primates; above all, of that primate of primates, *Homo sapiens*. The existence of this behavioural plasticity does not, however, preclude the existence of genetic diversity in populations, or the existence of genetically programmed behaviour mechanisms in individual organisms. Viewed in evolutionary perspective, therefore, learning behaviour is a phylogenetic adaptation, a way of completing the differentiation of the central nervous and related systems 'in greater detail and more adaptively than can be accomplished by gene encoding alone',[85] and it is this evolutionary innovation which has made possible the adaptive radiation which we observe in the diverse cultures of man.

A stage has now been reached, then, in the biological study of behaviour where any rigid and pervasive dichotomy between innate and acquired responses has become otiose. Galambos, in his recent discussion of the brain correlates of learning, has written: 'every sample of behaviour reveals an aspect of the past history of the organism that has been stored within the brain. These memories arise both via genes and through experience'; and he has suggested that 'all of them come into existence, are stored, and receive their expression through fundamentally the same mechanisms'.[86]

---

83   R.J. Dubos, *So Human an Animal* (New York, Scribner, 1968), p. 77.
84   W.R. Thompson, 'Influence of prenatal maternal anxiety on emotionality in young rats', *Science* (1957), 125:698–699; G. Gottlieb, 'Prenatal behavior in birds', *Quarterly Review of Biology* (1968), 43:148–174.
85   J.L. Fuller and W.R. Thompson, *Behavior Genetics* (New York, John Wiley, 1960), p. 4.
86   R. Galambos, 'Brain correlates of learning', in *The Neurosciences*, p. 641.

Thus, the discoveries of recent decades demand of the student of animal and human behaviour an interactionist paradigm which gives recognition to genetical and environmental feedback and interaction both in the ontogeny of individual organisms and in the phylogeny of breeding populations.

This interactionist paradigm, it will be seen, is markedly at variance with that contrived by Kroeber, Watson and the other intransigent environmentalists of the 1920s and 1930s, and its emergence has been the chief cause of the ferment that has been abroad in the behavioural sciences in recent years, and particularly since the advent of behaviour genetics in the early 1960s. Today, I would doubt it there are any informed behavioural scientists who would wish to take other than an interactionist position, and this must be ranked as one of the principal happenings in the scientific progress set in motion by the new biology.

Further, the interactionist paradigm has given rise to the exciting prospect of a unified science of man and his behaviour. For example, the recent major symposium on 'Biology and Behavior', held at Rockefeller University, had as its aim, according to Carl Pfaffman, the initiation of 'a period from which a unitary science of man will emerge in which his biochemistry, biophysics and biology will be integrated with the understanding of his behaviour'.[87]

As a result of this progress, and the present scientific supremacy of the interactionist paradigm, not a few social scientists and others, trained in yesteryear, now find themselves far out on a conceptual limb not of their own making — and this can no longer be regarded as a salubrious intellectual situation in which to be. In other words, such has been the progression in biological discovery and understanding during recent years that no one who professionally concerns himself with the study of men and their ways can afford any longer to pride himself on his illiteracy in matters biological. Rather, one would hope and expect that before long suitable courses on the evolutionary and biological bases of behaviour will become a recognised part of professional training in all disciplines in any way concerned with human behaviour.

---

87   C. Pfaffman, *Introduction to Neurophysiology and Emotion* (first of a series on Biology and Behavior, proceedings of a conference held under the auspices of the Russell Sage Foundation and the Rockefeller University), ed. David C. Glass (New York, Rockefeller University Press and Russell Sage Foundation, 1967), p. ix.

In recent years there have also been major changes in our understanding of the probable nature of human evolution. As I noted earlier, the cultural anthropologists of the early decades of this century would have no truck with Darwin's theory of evolution by natural selection. Thus, Kroeber, having asserted that 'nothing, homologous to the rudest culture' existed even among 'the highest animals', went on to advance the theory that culture had not evolved gradually in the course of human phylogenesis, but had originated by a sudden 'leap to another plane'.[88] The subsequent discoveries of prehistoric archaeology and of the ethological study of infra-human primate behaviour have reduced Kroeber's theory to the status of a private fantasy, for it is now known, from the researches of Dr Jane van Lawick-Goodall and others among wild chimpanzees in central Africa,[89] as also from those of Dr Kawai and his associates on the Japanese monkey,[90] that rudimentary cultural behaviour does indeed exist among infra-human primates; furthermore, both the palaeontological and archaeological evidence demonstrates an unbroken evolutionary continuity. Kroeber's theory, therefore, must be rejected, as also, on genetical grounds, must the Lamarckian theory of human domestication advanced by Boas.[91] From a multitude of scientific discoveries, then, it has become plain that evolution by natural selection has gradually created the human species, as it has all other populations of living things — but with certain innovations which seem to have occurred mainly in the evolutionary history of the *Hominidae* — that is of *Homo sapiens,* and the fossil species related to him.

And here I would like to pay tribute to the work of Sherwood Washburn, the distinguished American evolutionary anthropologist, whose researches and interpretations (with those of his many collaborators and colleagues) are leading to the emergence of a new anthropology. Among the most

---

88   Kroeber, 'The morals of uncivilized people', *American Anthropologist* (1910), 12:437; 'The superorganic', *American Anthropologist* (1917), 19:163–213; cf. p. 208; 'Social evolution is without antecedents in the beginnings of organic evolution … the dawn of the social thus is not a link in any chain, not a step in a path, but a leap to another plane'.

89   Lawick-Goodall, 'The behaviour of free-living chimpanzees in the Gombe stream reserve', pp. 202ff; A. Kortlandt and M. Kooij, Protohominid behaviour in primates', *Symposia of the Zoological Society of London* (1963), 10:61–88; Kortlandt, 'On tool-use among primates', *Current Anthropology* (1966), 7:215–216.

90   M. Kawai, 'Japanese monkeys and the origin of culture', *Animals* (1965), 5:450–455.

91   Boas, 'Human faculty as determined by race', pp. 309ff; *The Mind of Primitive Man*, pp. 75ff; 'The aims of anthropological research', *Science* (1932), 76:607.

important of Washburn's notions is the inference that the gene pools of hominid populations evolved in a feedback relationship with nascent cultural behaviour. Thus, in Washburn's words:

> The success of initial tool using, perhaps only slightly more advanced than that seen in the contemporary chimpanzee, led to selection for the biology that made tool using possible, and the study of the brain of *Homo sapiens* shows that large areas are associated with hand skills. The reason that tool making evolved so slowly was that the brain had to evolve before the skills of *Homo erectus* were anatomically possible. According to this view the explanation of human evolution is to be sought in the feedback relation between successful behaviour and the biology that makes the behaviour possible.[92]

In other words, a cultural innovation is an addition to the previously existing environment with consequent feedback or selective pressure on the breeding population and its gene pool; which means, it will be discerned, that instead of being 'utterly divergent', as Kroeber in his ignorance supposed, cultural behaviour and man's biological nature have, on repeated occasions in the unbroken course of evolution, been in communication at the molecular level, for, as J.B.S. Haldane has succinctly phrased it, 'the principal unit process in evolution is the substitution of one gene for another at the same locus'.[93]

We may say then that the species *Homo sapiens* is pre-eminently the evolutionary product of the new selective pressures that came with the emergence of rudimentary forms of culture — this emergence going back some millions of years, at least into the Pliocene, and possibly, as Leakey has recently suggested,[94] into the Miocene. It follows that, in the study of human evolution, prehistoric archaeology and the comparative analysis of cultural behaviour become as important as genetics, the neurosciences, ethology and ecology; and further, that the relevant concepts and findings of all these and various cognate sciences must be integrated if the aetiology of human evolution is to be fully comprehended.

---

92   S.L. Washburn, 'Behavior and the origin of man', *Rockefeller University Review* (1968), January–February, p. 17.

93   Haldane, 'The cost of natural selection', *Journal of Genetics* (1957), 55:511.

94   L.S.B. Leakey, 'Development of aggression as a factor in early human and pre-human evolution', in *Aggression and Defense* (*Brain Function*, Vol. 5) (Berkeley and Los Angeles, University of California Press, 1967), p. 7.

With the advent of cultural behaviour, then, our hominid ancestors entered a new phase of evolutionary development in which behavioural adaptations dependent on the transfer of information from generation to generation by other than wholly genetic mechanisms gradually increased, until, with the emergence of symbolic modes of communication, *Homo sapiens* has become that evolutionary *rara avis* — a predominantly cultural animal. Nonetheless, as modern research indicates, our capacity to increase and transmit learned behaviour is still and always has been and will be ultimately dependent on phylogenetically evolved capacities. It thus becomes apparent that culture is a purely natural phenomenon, and has developed in continuous interaction with phylogenetic processes to become the prime biological adaptation of our species.

It is, moreover, our unique evolutionary history which has made us the 'embodied paradox' that we are; for man, in behavioural terms, is a kind of evolutionary compendium, with mechanisms in the phylogenetically old parts of his brain, such as his reticular formation and limbic system, which he shares with vertebrates as meagre as lizards and as excitable as the chimpanzee; while in his neo-cortex are neuronal circuits which confer on him the capacity to engage in symbolic behaviour and to exercise preferences — so that he becomes like a god, having knowledge of good and evil. This capacity to exercise preferences has gradually emerged in the course of human evolution in close conjunction with the capacity to symbolise, to recall the past and envisage the future, and so has given to man a freedom of action, limited though it be by inexorable natural processes, that far excels that of any other animal organism. And with this freedom — as the brief chronicle of our recorded history shows — human individuals have soared to sublime heights and descended to disastrous depths.

We are here confronted with the phenomenon of human values, for values are a function of the capacity to exercise preferences, and so, ineluctably become a part of the subject matter of evolutionary anthropology, as indeed of any discipline that concerns itself with human behaviour.

In the words of the American biologist Herrick: 'Man's capacity for intelligently directed self-development confers on him the ability to determine the pattern of his culture and so to shape the course of human evolution in directions of his own choice. This ability, which no other animals have, is man's most distinctive characteristic, and it is, perhaps, the most significant fact known to science.'[95]

The truth embodied in these words has now, I believe, become apparent to very many scientists; moreover, concern with values is intrinsic to what Bronowski has called 'the culture of science'. We can practise science, as Bronowski reminds us, 'only if we value the truth'.[96] By valuing the truth, scientists make radical discoveries about the determinisms of nature, which inevitably extend the range of choices open to men, and so create situations in which concern with values is inescapable. Indeed, I would argue that it is only when he understands something of the determinisms of nature, including, most importantly, the determinisms of his own body and brain, that a man can begin to become truly and humanly free. As René Dubos has so well expressed it: 'Man makes himself through enlightened choices that enhance his humanness'.[97]

What then are the prospects for a science of human values? First, it will be necessary to transcend the doctrine of cultural relativism which denies even the possibility of any broadly based evaluation of human choices, by asserting, as it does, that differing forms of cultural behaviour or shared preference are normal *sui generis,* and so cannot be compared in biogenetic or any other terms.

Fortunately, the biological sciences have something better to offer us. Basic to the science of evolutionary biology is the phenomenon and concept of adaptation. Simpson, Pittendrigh and Tiffany have defined an adaptation as 'any aspect of the organism which promotes its welfare, or the general welfare of the species to which it belongs, in the environment it usually inhabits'.[98] Fundamental to this definition is the notion of welfare, and it is apparent, in the light of much cumulative experience in the biological sciences, that no adequate analysis of the evolutionary process is possible without the concept of adaptive value.

---

95 C.J. Herrick, cited by Robert B. Livingston in *The Neurosciences*, p. 500.
96 J. Bronowski, *The Identity of Man* (New York, Natural History Press, 1965), p. 100.
97 Dubos, *So Human an Animal*, p. xii.
98 G.G. Simpson, C.S. Pittendrigh and L.H. Tiffany, *Life: an Introduction to Biology* (New York, Harcourt, Brace, 1957), p. 434.

Further, concomitant with this fundamental biological phenomenon of adaptation is the phenomenon of organic diversity, for adaptation and diversity are equally the products of evolution by natural selection. Moreover, this diversity of animals and their behaviour exists both among species and between individuals within the same Mendelian population.

From these natural characteristics of populations of living things, we are able to derive the fundamental principle of *adaptive diversity*, and it is this principle, I would suggest, that must guide any science of human values, for it provides us with the soundest of biological foundations — *the positive evaluation of diversity whenever it is adaptive* — this being the value inherent in evolution by natural selection and so in the life process itself.

The analysis of the diversities of human behaviour in terms of their adaptive value must depend, it is plain, on a unified scientific understanding of the natures and situations of human beings. This scientific understanding, which we have been seeking for so short a time, is still very limited, but it is now progressing faster and more fundamentally than ever before in our extraordinary history as a species, and from this we can take hope.

But let us also hope that those who become involved in the scientific study of values will not neglect the wisdom of their precursors, who, down the ages, have given concern to the nature — ever-changing as it is — of human values.

On a wall of one of Canberra's high schools someone has written: God is dead. Beneath it a juvenile wit has added the words: No, he's not, he's alive, and doing a science course at the Uni. This experience, I have little doubt, would be edifying to many of the gods of which men have so far conceived, but I am constrained to wonder whether some of man's gods, if only in the sense of symbolic projections of species' wisdom about adaptive values, might not have something of importance to tell some of the scientists.

One of the most memorable of William Blake's poems begins:

> *Tyger! Tyger! burning bright*
> *In the forests of the night.*
> *What immortal hand or eye*
> *Could frame thy fearful symmetry?*

And Blake goes on to ask:

Did he who made the Lamb make thee?

We now know that it was the evolutionary process that made the Tyger burning bright, as it made us; but to me as a student of human evolution, one of the most notable of evolutionary phenomena is that the human species, ascended as it is from impulsive, predatory and carnivorous apes, should have produced behavioural innovators, whatever their quirks, such as Hammurabi and Confucius, Akenaton and the Buddha, Jesus (for Blake's Lamb has a capital L) and Francis of Assisi, who, with his awareness of the interdependence of living things, might well be adopted (as an American historian has recently suggested)[99] as the patron saint of ecology.

Such an ethic of concern for the welfare of others, which is comparable to the Buddhist value of needfulness, is gradually becoming part of a scientific and humanistic attitude towards human existence, and a true scientist must, I believe, while not abandoning the mechanistic *Weltanschauung* (which has contributed so markedly to the scientific understanding of biological phenomena), come to adopt such an attitude of informed concern towards the life process in all its aspects, for without such human values, as W.H. Auden has reminded us, 'no secular wall will safely stand'.[100]

What we can rationally hope for, then, is the emergence, within the next few decades, of a unified science of man and his behaviour, grounded on evolutionary biology, and drawing on the universe of relevant scientific knowledge, while remaining cognisant of evolving human values in their adaptive diversity.

When geneticists, neuroscientists, ethologists and ecologists can sit down with archaeologists and historians, psychologists and anthropologists, to work together, using a common scientific and human language, to illumine the evolutionary history and the natures and cultures of men, the day of such a unified science of man will have dawned. That day, I hope and believe, is not far distant.

---

99   L. White, 'The historical roots of our ecologic crisis', *Science* (1967), 155:1207.
100 W.H. Auden, 'Vespers' in *Collected Shorter Poems, 1927–1957* (London, Faber and Faber, 1966), p. 335.

CHAPTER 2

The Anthropology of Choice[1]

I greatly appreciate having been invited to speak to the anthropology, archaeology and linguistics sections of the 49th ANZAAS Congress. For me there is a satisfaction in returning to New Zealand, for although I am now an Australian citizen and on the academic staff of an Australian university, I began my life in these islands, with my study of anthropology in the late 1930s at Victoria University College (as it then was) being under the guidance of Ernest Beaglehole.

Beaglehole, having taken his PhD in London, under Morris Ginsberg, had gone on to study anthropology at Yale University with Edward Sapir, one of the founders of modern linguistic anthropology who had himself been a student of Franz Boas. From Yale, Beaglehole did fieldwork among the Hopi, and then in Hawaii and Pukapuka before joining Victoria University College in 1937. As one of his students, I was soon introduced to anthropology, and in 1938 in the student paper *Salient* (which I had helped to found) there appeared my first anthropological article. It was entitled 'Anatomy of Mind', argued that the human mind was 'a social product', and was illustrated, alack, with a cartoon in which an individual, standing haplessly in the hinder part of a pantomime horse was being told that he was merely the 'product of his environment'.

As this indicates, cultural determinism was, at that time, very much in vogue, and, understandably enough, one of the books that I had with me in Western Samoa at the beginning of the 1940s, when I first tried my hand at anthropological enquiry, was the late Margaret Mead's *From the South Seas*, which contained the study for which she is still most widely known: *Coming of Age in Samoa*.

---

1   An ANZAAS Presidential Address given in Auckland, New Zealand, on 24 January 1979.

As Margaret Mead noted in her preface to *From the South Seas*, the issue 'uppermost in the minds of the scientific world' during the years 1926 to 1928 when she wrote *Coming of Age in Samoa* was: 'What is human nature?'

In 1924, at the height of the Nature–Nurture controversy, Franz Boas, in an article in the *American Mercury*, had pointed to the fundamental need for a detailed investigation of hereditary and environmental conditions. And, the following year, he sent Margaret Mead to Samoa to study 'the extent to which the well-known vicissitudes of adolescents' were 'dependent upon the physical changes through which they were passing or upon the nature of the culture within which they grew up'. It was Boas's view that 'the social stimulus' was 'infinitely more potent' than 'biological mechanism'. In the thirteenth chapter of *Coming of Age in Samoa*, Margaret Mead went even further, claiming, on the basis of her enquiries into adolescence in Samoa, that explanations other than in terms of environmental factors could not be made. This conclusion (which in my view is most certainly not substantiated by the Samoan evidence) was taken up with alacrity by many other anthropologists and soon became central to the widely popular anthropological doctrine in which human nature and behaviour are explained 'in purely cultural terms'.

In September 1978, just half a century after the first appearance of *Coming of Age in Samoa*, there was published, by Harvard University Press, a book heralded as initiating 'a new phase in the most important intellectual controversy' of our times. It was E.O. Wilson's *On Human Nature*, and the controversy, as in the 1920s, is still about Nature and Nurture.

In the opening lines of the first paragraph of this provocative addition to the literature of philosophical anthropology, Wilson poses a question which, as he notes, was judged by Hume to be of 'unspeakable importance'. Significantly, it is the very question — 'What is Man's ultimate nature?' — to which Margaret Mead supposed she had provided a quite conclusive answer in 1928. The answer that Wilson gives to this question is virtually antithetical to that offered by Mead, for although he does recognise the existence of cultural evolution, the essence of his sociobiological argument is that 'the brain exists because it promotes the survival and multiplication of the genes that direct its assembly', from which it follows that 'biology is the key to human nature'.

And so, today, as in the 1920s, the study of Man remains deeply riven. On the one hand, as Stephen Toulmin has recently put it, are those who 'see all human behaviour as one more phenomenon of Nature: who are concerned, that is, to discover in human behaviour only "general laws", dependent on universal ahistorical processes and so free of all cultural variability'. And on the other hand, there are those who 'see Culture as a distinct and entirely autonomous field of study set over against Nature: a field within which diversity and variety are the rule and "general laws" are not to be looked for'.

Like Toulmin, I find this conceptual polarization 'a depressing prospect'. It is a polarisation that will not be transcended until we succeed in establishing, in an evolutionary perspective, the nature of the linkages between biology and culture. My thesis is that one of the most fundamental of these linkages is to be found in human choice behaviour which, as I shall argue, is both intrinsic to our biology and basic to the very formation of cultures.

In *The Selfish Gene* (published in 1976) Richard Dawkins, the Oxford ethologist, deploying sociobiological theory, has argued that human beings, like other animals, are 'machines' created by their genes during millions of years of evolution by means of natural selection. This general view, we must, I think, accept, for, as Dawkins remarks, 'today, the theory of evolution is about as much open to doubt as the theory that the earth goes round the sun'. Yet, as Dawkins himself goes on to admit, there is, in the case of the human species, a crucial limit to the determinative potency of our genes. Thus, in the final two sentences of his book he tells us that humans, alone on earth, are in possession of a 'power' that enables them to 'rebel' against the 'tyranny' of their genes, the 'selfish replicators' of sociobiology.

After all that the sociobiologists have told us of the immense potency of the 'genetic rules of human nature' (to use one of E.O. Wilson's phrases), any 'power' able, as Dawkins admits, to overcome the 'tyranny' of these 'genetic rules' must be formidable indeed. And so, it was with some curiosity that I wrote to Dawkins asking him how he would describe this remarkable and uniquely human power, and putting it to him that what he was referring to could only be, as far as I could see, the human capacity to make choices.

'I cannot disagree with you,' Dawkins replied, 'I am referring to the human capacity to make choices'; and he then went on to add that he suspected that 'the difference between man and other animals' in their choice-making capacities was 'a quantitative difference in amount of complexity'.

Let this then be our starting point: the fact that members of the human species possess a capacity to make choices which, while it is developed to an extent that clearly distinguishes them from other animals, is nonetheless a capacity, biological in origin, which other animals, to a lesser extent, also possess.

This evolutionary fact, I shall argue, is of quite fundamental significance for anthropology, for, when the capacity to make choices is recognised as a biological phenomenon in terms of which we can account for the emergence of human cultures, we can then transcend the primitive, sectarian and unscientific doctrine that culture is 'a thing *sui generis*', a 'superorganic' and 'closed' system in no communication whatsoever with biology.

When he first advanced this doctrine, in the *American Anthropologist* in 1917, Kroeber argued that biology and cultural anthropology were separated by an unbridgeable chasm. Kroeber, it is now apparent, was mistaken in this assertion, for the findings of palaeo-anthropology and archaeology during recent decades have made it abundantly clear that the emergence of human culture is very definitely an evolutionary phenomenon. And this means that in recognising a continuity between genetic and cultural evolution we must also, in our theoretical formulations, attempt to identify the mechanisms that facilitated the emergence of cultural adaptations. It is precisely here, in my judgement, that the human capacity to make choices is of such crucial significance.

In advancing this view, I am, I would note, building on foundations laid by others. For example, in their book *Prehistoric Societies*, first published in 1965, Grahame Clark and Stuart Piggott noted that 'social evolution differed from biological evolution in allowing for the first time an element of conscious choice both to social groups and to individuals'. And, in 1969, Sherwood Washburn concluded his paper 'The Evolution of Human Behaviour' with the words: 'The human way of life maximizes adaptation through awareness and choice, and these abilities depend on human biology'.

Fundamental to my whole argument is Washburn's conclusion that the human capacity to make choices stems from our biology. Thus, accepting scientific materialism, in the same sense as does E.O. Wilson, I am arguing that the human capacity to make choices is phylogenetically given, and so, an entirely natural phenomenon.

In other words, I am suggesting that choice behaviour is part of the human ethogram, as it is of the ethograms of various of the higher animals — a conclusion, I would add, that is in accord with the views of Charles Darwin, who, in his *The Descent of Man*, lists choice as one of the 'faculties' to be found in animals as well as in humans.

Let us then glance, for a moment, at choice behaviour in infra-human animals, it being integral to my argument that the highly developed human capacity to make choices has evolutionary antecedents in the more rudimentary choice behaviour of animals lower in the phylogenetic scale.

Choice, in its basic sense, is a process in which a selection is made between alternatives. And this process, through the operation of some specific mechanism, would seem to be fundamental to the behaviour of virtually all animals. I would particularly emphasise, once again, that the approach I am making to human choice behaviour is strictly within a scientific and naturalistic frame of reference. Accordingly, I am viewing the action of choosing between alternatives as an entirely natural phenomenon, and I do not suppose that humans, in the choices they make, are any more able to depart from the determinisms of Nature than are other animals.

As long ago as 1933, H.S. Jennings, the American microbiologist, observed that 'life is a continuous process of selecting one line of action and rejecting another', and that this applied to all animals, including one-celled organisms. Since then, this fact has been demonstrated in numerous experimental studies, including experiments on the behaviour of such lowly organisms as paramecia, planaria and meal worms.

Recently, indeed, William Baum, writing of animal organisms in general, has advanced as 'fundamental' the proposition that 'all behaviour constitutes choice, because in any set of environmental conditions several alternative activities can occur'.

In studying the process whereby an animal chooses between alternatives, the investigator contrives what is called a 'choice situation', this being an experimentally controlled situation in which it is possible to make more than one response. From such studies a wide range of 'choices' on the part of animals has now been demonstrated. For example, in a study in which goldfish were exposed to young piranha fish, the piranha showed a marked 'preference' (in 87.9 per cent of trials) to attack the tail area of their prey (Foxx 1972:280). Armadillos, pigeons and cats, in contrast to pigs, goats and humans, have been shown to lack any 'preference' for sweet substances (Kennedy and Baldwin 1972:706). Hens 'given a choice of spending 8–16 hours in a space rather smaller or alternatively considerably larger than that afforded by their home cage prefer the larger space' (Hughes 1975:563). And laboratory rats given a 'choice' between bar-pressing for food, or taking it freely from a dish, greatly prefer to 'freeload' (Tarte and Snyder 1973:128 et seq.).

While explicitly referring to the behaviour of their experimental animals in terms of 'choice' and 'preference', the investigators tend to interpret these selections between alternatives as being wholly or predominantly genetic adaptations. That is, it is concluded that the members of the species concerned have been evolved by natural selection to make fixed 'choices' among the alternatives they commonly encounter in their environments. In some instances, learning and intelligence are also clearly involved; however, all that I want to establish, at this stage of my argument, is that choice behaviour, in the sense that one alternative is preferred (by whatever mechanism) to another, is characteristic of a wide range of infra-human animals.

While very many of the selections between alternatives that animals make appear to be genetically determined, there is also to be found among higher animals various kinds of intelligent behaviour in which the making of choices is a means to an appetitive end. Such choices may be termed instrumental. For example, from experiments with T mazes there have been repeated demonstrations that 'rats will learn to choose consistently the alternative leading to the larger of two rewards' (Hill and Spear 1963:723). In other words, in a T maze a hungry rat will exercise choice in such a way as to maximise its intake of food.

Again, numerous experiments have shown that chimpanzees are well capable of the instrumental use of choice when appetitively aroused. Wolfgang Kohler, in his classic book *The Mentality of Apes*, records many instances of choice behaviour of this kind. For example, when the male chimpanzee Sultan was set a test in which he had to choose between a graph of an empty wooden box and a photograph of the same box containing bananas, he 'rapidly succeeded', Kohler reports, 'in choosing correctly in about ninety out of every hundred occasions'. In a more recent experiment, at the University of Munster in West Germany, when two of six tools which were known to a female chimpanzee were offered to her, with only one of the pair being a possible means of obtaining food, she chose the correct tool in 238 out of 250 trials — a success rate of about 95 per cent (J. Döhl 1969:200 et seq.).

Instrumental choice behaviour is especially characteristic of primates, and there is now substantial evidence on its crucial role in infra-human culture formation — as, for example, among free-ranging Japanese macaques. In September 1953, on Koshima Island, a female macaque called F-111, about 15 months old, was observed to carry a sand-covered sweet potato to a stream, where she washed it in water, in both hands, before eating it. In so behaving, she was selecting, for the first time in the evolutionary history of Japanese macaques, a quite novel alternative. Precisely how F-111 first discovered that sand could be washed from sweet potato in this way is not known, but almost certainly it was in the course of play, which is closely akin to imagination. What is known for certain is that, having hit upon this specific alternative, she continued to select it. By February 1954, three other monkeys had learned to imitate F-111's innovative choice, and ten years later 74 per cent of the troop of 59 monkeys had, one by one, made the alternative of washing sweet potatoes a part of their behavioural repertoire, and so a part of the 'culture' of the Koshima macaques.

This well-attested historical sequence is of profound theoretical interest, for it clearly indicates the fundamentals of the process of culture formation in infra-human primates. The process begins by the chance discovery, usually by a single individual, of a new and feasible behavioural alternative; this alternative is then selected so that it becomes a part of this individual's behavioural repertoire; next, the selected alternative is imitatively selected by other individuals until it gradually becomes a widely shared behaviour within their social group; after which it continues to be transmitted, from generation to generation, by way of imitative learning.

It will be discerned that we are here dealing with a process in which behavioural selection or choice is instrumental in bringing into being a new mode of behaviour, the survival of which depends not on any genetic adaptation but on the mechanisms of social learning. Moreover, although the mechanisms involved are decidedly different from those of genetic evolution, the processes of culture formation (as illustrated by the Koshima example) are every bit as much a part of Nature. We are dealing, in fact, with another kind of natural selection, which, because the mechanisms involved are so different from those of genetics, we must recognise as being, in fact, a second evolutionary system.

Among Japanese macaques this second evolutionary system, which is dependent, as we have seen, on instrumental choice and imitative learning, remains of quite minor importance. Nonetheless, the fact that it is to be found among contemporary infra-human primates is of radical anthropological significance for it enables us to infer that choice and imitative behaviour of at least a comparable kind was characteristic of the hominids, at the time, say, of *Homo habilis*, about 1.75 million years ago.

That this was the case is confirmed by the fact that *Homo habilis* possessed stone tools. As Clark and Piggott have remarked: 'Man's earliest essays in culture are best traced through his artifacts of flint and other kinds of stone'; that is, by what Clark and Piggott have appropriately called 'cultural fossils'.

This concept of a 'cultural fossil' is highly pertinent to my theme, for it refers to artifacts that are quite distinct from the zoological and other fossils that taxonomists classify as the products of the first or genetic evolutionary system; to artifacts, that is, which are due not to the operation of genetic mechanisms but to the innovative behaviour of a hominid; or, to be more precise, to instrumental choice behaviour, for such artifacts can only have resulted from the selection, by their makers, of certain specific alternatives.

We are here at a momentous turning-point in evolutionary history at which a primate, by the intelligent manipulation of possibility, unknowingly embarked on a course that has ended in his becoming that most odd of all Nature's quirks, a predominantly rational animal; one who, whether he likes it or not, has a highly developed capacity for alternative action, and so is, to give a new twist to Aeschylus' words, a 'steersman of necessity'. From this crucial stage in human history, then, we must, as Richard Dawkins has put it, throw out the gene as 'the sole basis of our ideas on evolution'; which means, of course, that from this stage onwards the competence of sociobiological theory to account fully for human evolution comes decisively to an end.

Thus, while genetic evolution actively continues, it is accompanied, from this time onwards, by a new or second evolutionary system, based on different mechanisms, so that from the beginning of the Palaeolithic the genus *Homo*, to use E.O. Wilson's words, has moved on a 'dual track of evolution', with two clearly distinguishable evolutionary systems — the one genetic and the other cultural — in regular interaction.

Furthermore, while at the outset of this 'dual track' the first or genetic system was very predominantly important, this situation, throughout the Lower and Middle Palaeolithic, very gradually changed; and, during the Upper Palaeolithic and particularly since the Neolithic, has been reversed, with the result that from about the time of the invention of writing at the end of the fourth millennium BC cultural evolution has been as predominant in human history as was, formerly, the genetic system.

E.O. Wilson has recently argued that human nature, in its essentials, is the 'legacy' of the 'selection pressures of hunter-gatherer existence', which, extending from the time of, say, *Homo habilis* to the Neolithic, accounts for more than 99 per cent of the 'dual track' of human evolution. Accepting that these selection pressures were indeed of decisive importance, let us consider what the nature of this 'legacy' is likely to have been.

Our best measure of what happened within the 'dual track' of human evolution during the vast length of the Palaeolithic is, as I have already noted, its 'cultural fossils' — as, for example, the hand-axes of the Middle Pleistocene. In discussing a major sequence of these hand-axes (obtained from successive levels through Beds II to IV in the Olduvai Gorge), Clark and Piggott observe that it clearly shows 'how by insensible gradations, handier, and incidentally, more beautiful, tools with smoother working edges were produced from a smaller amount of raw material'.

In these gradations we have an example of how a set of alternatives, having been discovered and then selected to become part of the culture of early man, is both maintained and steadily improved. Up to a point, as Clark and Piggott remark, 'improvement could be made by acquiring greater skill in the use of a hammerstone', but 'no marked or rapid advance' was possible until some individual 'had the idea' (or, as I would prefer to say, selected the alternative) of 'using a punch of wood or bone and striking this sharply at right-angles'. By this means 'it was possible to detach thinner flakes having shallower bulbs of percussion than those removed by hammerstones; and the intersection of shallower flakes produced a more regular working edge'.

The gradual selection, by imitation, of this technical improvement can be traced in the archaeological record, and the whole process, from the initial innovation to its social adoption, would seem to be virtually identical with the instance of culture formation in a troop of Japanese macaques, which I have already discussed. In each instance choice behaviour, as evinced in the taking up of alternatives, is centrally involved.

In the ease of early man, with his gathering and hunting economy in which individual and group survival came to depend on the possession of effective stone tools, there would have been a strong selective pressure for the evolution, through genetic mechanisms, of the biological capacities required for the maintenance and improvement of his stone and related technologies. In this way, then, there would have been, throughout the Palaeolithic, a feedback relation, within the 'dual track' of human evolution, between any successful behaviour and the biology that made this behaviour possible. That this is what did occur is evidenced by the changes that occurred in the size and complexity of the brain: and in the archaeological record, in which, throughout the Palaeolithic, the capacity of early man to 'accumulate improvements' in the taking up of newly devised alternatives is displayed, as Clark and Piggott note, in the elaboration and refinement of his stone and other tools.

The basic process, I would argue, was one in which cultural innovations contribute to the generation of selective pressures that result in adaptive changes in human biology. I am inclined then to conclude, following Clark, Piggott and Washburn, that the nascent capacities to imagine and to choose between alternatives that were present among early hominids continued to develop during the ensuing millennia of gathering and hunting. Further, in addition to the kinds of process I have already described in discussing the cultural evolution of stone tools, there were the general demands of a gathering and hunting way of life.

As Laughlin has noted, hunting 'involves goals and motivations tor which intricate inhibition systems have developed' and places 'a premium' on 'inventiveness' and upon 'problem-solving'. And gathering, certainly, involves an incessant process of picking and choosing. Indeed, when one ponders the name that Linneaus conferred on our species in 1758, it has an oddly appropriate evolutionary sense, for *sapiens* is derived from the Latin *sapere*, which refers to discrimination in tasting, and so, ultimately, to the choosing behaviour of our Palaeolithic ancestors.

It is my hypothesis, then, that a principal 'legacy' of the 'selection pressures of hunter gatherer existence' was the cumulative evolutionary development in human biology of the capacities to imagine and to choose between alternatives. I would also suppose that it was the evolutionary developments of these capacities, together with the formation of elaborated languages, that, with other things, made possible the remarkable advance in cultural evolution that occurred from about 40,000 BC onwards.

Washburn has recently suggested that while man 'was surely not mute for most of his development', the 'critical new factor' that provided 'a biological base' for 'the acceleration of history' from about 40,000 years ago onwards, was 'the development of speech as we know it today'. This view is very much in accord with the conclusions of Isaac, who infers, from the available archaeological evidence, that while 'the milieu in which capabilities for language were first important began more than a million years ago, crucial developments in language took place about 40,000 to 30,000 BC; and it would seem likely, as Washburn has proposed, that 'just as upright walking and tool-making were the unique adaptation of the earlier phases of human evolution, so was the physiological capacity for speech the biological basis for the later stages'.

Of the crucial importance of effective languages in these later stages of human prehistory there can be no doubt. What a spoken language provides, with its uniquely human phonetic code, is an extraordinarily potent means of generating new information, a feature which has been well described by E.O. Wilson:

> In any language words are given arbitrary definitions within each culture and ordered according to a grammar that imparts new meaning above and beyond the definitions. The full symbolic quality of the words and the sophistication of the grammar permit the creation of messages that are potentially infinite in number.

This means that all human languages possess what Steiner has called alternity; that is, they immensely facilitate the conceptualising of possibilities not previously perceived and so generate new alternatives from which choices can be made. With the development of effective languages, then, the second evolutionary system of human populations was transformed, for it was now possible to supplement the observational learning that first gave rise to traditions with a highly efficient symbolic code in which cultural information of all kinds could be stored and transmitted from generation to generation. Man had become a *zoon phonanta* or language animal, and from the time of the effective completion of this transformation, about 40,000 years ago, his evolutionary history has been mainly cultural. The anthropological significance of this final stage of Man's gradual transition from a preponderantly genetic to a preponderantly cultural mode of evolution is difficult to exaggerate, and E.O. Wilson may well be justified in claiming that the development of human speech represented 'a quantum jump in evolution comparable to the assembly of the eucaryotic cell'.

From about 40,000 BC onwards, certainly, the Advanced Palaeolithic peoples began to explore an ever-extending range of new alternatives, and, towards the end of the Old Stone Age, there was, in the words of Jacquetta Hawkes, a 'sudden emergence of full human creativity' that ranks as 'one of the most astonishing chapters' in all human history, 'It is evident,' Jacquetta Hawkes comments, 'that after hundreds of thousands of years during which the people of each generation normally did exactly what their parents had done and cultural improvement was extremely slow,' the Advanced Palaeolithic peoples had begun to 'think in terms of solving problems'. The evidence for this is a remarkable series of inventions such as the spear-thrower, the harpoon and the eyed-needle, and works of art — all of which I would interpret as having resulted from capacities of imagination and choice which, with the rapid development of language, had suddenly become markedly more effective.

Again, beginning during the Epipalaeolithic and Neolithic periods in the Near East, there was an extraordinary efflorescence of human agency in which a bewildering range of new alternatives was taken up as the numerous civilisations of that region began to form. In contrast to the extreme gradualness of change in the Middle Pleistocene, the human capacity for alternative action was now producing an unending stream of diverse innovations. Indeed, with understandable hyperbole Clark and Piggott have described this process as having been 'infinitely variable'.

Although our evidence is largely inferential, I would suppose that these innovations also extended to human behaviour, and that as new alternatives, good and bad, were taken up in profusion, it became increasingly necessary to devise ethical and legal codes (such as that of Hammurabi, which dates from about 1750 BC) in an attempt to control human conduct as it became ever more imaginatively resourceful — a still-continuing process in human history, as those who have studied computer crime will know. It is in this same historical context, incidentally, that I would interpret the primeval myth of our civilisation concerning 'the tree of knowledge of good and evil'. Eve and Adam 'fell' because they chose the alternative of not conforming with God's command; which can only mean that they were created with choice behaviour as part of their natures — a form of behaviour so potent, with all, as to outstrip, in the twinkling of an eye, the omnipotence of the Creator himself.

There can really be no doubt, then, that choice, as Kierkegaard once remarked, is 'the most tremendous thing which has been granted to man', for it gives him the power to imitate, if he so decides, either god or devil, and then, should his imagination be sufficiently fecund, to outdo either of them.

It was, I would suppose, this same terrible yet splendid truth about the potential scope of human action of which Epictetus, the Stoic philosopher, was thinking when he remarked that 'nothing but itself can conquer Choice', an aphorism that must surely be most galling to any self-respecting 'selfish gene'.

Such then is the human capacity to make choices, and Kierkegaard's estimate of its tremendousness holds, I would observe, even if one attributes its presence in humans not to a Creator God, but to biological evolution, as do I.

Although it had probably existed from some tens of thousands of years previously, our first substantive evidence of the existence of preferential choice behaviour — that is, choice behaviour characterised by a fully conscious consideration of alternatives — is contained in Egyptian inscriptions of about 3400 BC in which 'some conduct is approved and some disapproved'. Evidence of a comparable kind is to be found in early Sumerian texts, such as the *Instructions of Suruppak*, which date from about 2500 BC, as in numerous other texts from this time onwards.

In the Torah of the nomadic Hebrews, for example, dating from about the 13th century BC, Yahweh is depicted (as I have already mentioned) as setting before his 'chosen people' alternatives of 'good' and 'evil', and then requiring of them that they should enter into a covenant with him to choose as he would have them choose.

As this historically important example reveals, virtually all human laws and rules (from wherever derived) are essentially socially preferred alternatives that have been instituted with the intention, as H.L.A. Hart has felicitously phrased it, of withdrawing certain kinds of conduct 'from the free option of the individual to do as he likes'. And of all the animals, I would add, only *Homo sapiens*, with his highly evolved capacity for alternative action, has any use for these codes of prohibited alternatives, as also, alas, the penchant endlessly to compile them.

During the 6th century BC a variety of other major ethical systems, including Zoroastrianism, Jainism, Buddhism, Taoism and Confucianism, came into existence, all of them based, as are all human value systems, on the notion of choice between humanly realisable alternatives. And from this same century there is abundant evidence of preferential choice behaviour in texts which have survived from archaic Greece.

So we find Alcaeus of Lesbos, who was a friend of Sappho, writing in about 600 BC:

> *Not houses finely roofed,*
> *nor the stones of walls well built.*
> *nor canals, not dockyards,*
> *make the city, but men able to use opportunity.*

While Sappho herself has this to say in one of her touchingly direct poems:

> *This way, that way,*
> *I do not know*
> *what to do: I*
> *am of two minds.*

And Theognis, in one of his Elegies, writing in the mid-6th century BC, tells us with the passionate existential anxiety of a character from a novel by Sartre:

> *As, for me,*
> *I'm wretched, torn apart and of two minds,*
> *I'm standing at the cross-road wondering*
> *which of two paths to take.*

Here then, in archaic Greece, almost a century before the birth of Socrates, stands modern man, bereft of the blind certainty of both fixed action patterns and divinely sanctioned ritual, having — as both evolution and Prometheus would have it — no choice but to learn to choose for himself. Further, there was also, among the archaic Greeks, a keen awareness of the crucially determinative nature of human choices; as, for example, in Hieroclis' 'Golden Verses' of Pythagoras (whose Apollonian community flourished in what is now southern Italy in the late 6th century BC) in which there occurs the line:

You will see that the evils that devour
men are the fruit of their choice.

These insights from the archaic period were explicated in detail by the great Greek philosophers of later centuries. As Xenophon tells us, Socrates thought that 'everyone acts by choosing from the courses open to him', and it was in this Socratic tradition that Aristotle embarked on his penetrating analysis of *proairesis*, or preferential choice, versions of which are to be found in both the Eudemian and the Nicomachaen Ethics.

Aristotle defines choice as 'taking one thing in preference to another', noting that 'this cannot be done without deliberation'. Furthermore, it is from deliberative choice, according to Aristotle, that human rationality springs. This, as Antony Flew has recently pointed out, is a conclusion of fundamental importance. In the light of evolutionary theory it means that rationality, like choice itself, is seen as a biologically based, emergent capacity of the human animal. It is also, I would add, very much in accord with the findings of modern research on intelligence. Colby, for example, has recently described intelligence as being, basically, a 'capacity to select the best action for a particular situation', which means that choosing between alternatives is always involved.

It was also Aristotle's view that rational, deliberative choice, which he regarded as 'the defining characteristic of human beings', was a nascent power that develops only with the acquisition of language and thought. It is thus lacking in infants and young children, as it is in infra-human animals.

This observation is, in my view, of the deepest significance for the student of human nature and of human evolution, for we here have a situation in which we may study the continuing interaction in human life of the first and second evolutionary systems.

Human infants enter this world as the unadorned products of genetic processes, with a limited range of behaviours that are sufficient, with adequate care, for their initial survival and subsequent development. Yet, utterly innocent, as they are, of any of the complex information that is transmitted within human societies by exogenetic mechanisms, they are still only human beings in embryo. What then ensues, after primary bonding has been established, is a prodigiously complex developmental process in which, as the researches of Vygotsky, Luria and other Russian psychologists have shown, the linguistically coded information of culture interacts with the infant's biological mechanisms to produce, by about five years of age, cortical structures that are basic to the higher psychological functions of a human being and which make further, and advanced, learning possible.

This is all very understandable in evolutionary terms, for, probably for well over 40,000 years, human cultural development has depended specifically on the learning and teaching of linguistically coded information; and, so much so, that, as S.A. Barnett has pointed out, our species, in zoological perspective, may be most appropriately described as consisting of creatures who actively teach their young, and may be named, accordingly, *Homo docens*.

I am, then, in agreement with Stephen Toulmin that it is in precisely this remarkable and far from fully understood developmental process that anthropologists and others, following the lead of Vygotsky, might most usefully study further the interaction of the genetic and exogenetic evolutionary systems in the hope of attaining an integrated understanding of the interrelation of nature and culture.

Aristotle's view that the 'capacity to originate action by choice' is 'the defining characteristic of human beings', although shared by many other thinkers, has been largely ignored by anthropologists; and especially by those for whom customary behaviour looms large, like the social anthropologist whom I once heard remarking on how satisfying it would be to do fieldwork in a society in which everybody behaved in exactly the same way.

In one of the lectures, preparatory to Greats, that he gave in Oxford, Gilbert Murray used to tell his listeners that:

> One of the great lessons which anthropology has taught us is the overpowering influence on mankind of tradition and tribal customs, of inherited taboos and superstitions.

He then went on to describe this conclusion as anthropology's 'depressing cordial'.

That many humans are prone, as the researches of Milgram and others have shown, to accept information on authority and unreflectively is undeniably true. But there is also a highly invigorating cordial that anthropology has to offer; for throughout human history there have always been those who have questioned tradition, and who have taken action, often courageously, to bring about humanly valuable changes. The very fact that this has occurred demonstrates to us that a culture is essentially a socially sanctioned accumulation of alternatives that have been selected from the vast range of human possibility. And, this being so, it is always possible for those involved to change in some way, or abandon, one or more of the alternatives of their culture.

And it is this same situation, I would add, that invalidates the once popular doctrine of cultural relativism which maintains that human cultures, varying as they do, are not open to any kind of critical evaluation. In fact, human cultures vary as they do precisely because it is possible for human populations to choose between alternatives. But choice, in contrast to natural selection, is by no means necessarily adaptive, for when made in ignorance a choice may have unforeseen consequences of a highly deleterious kind.

And so, as Washburn and McCown have noted, 'major human misconceptions are built into the basis of every cultural system'; from which it follows, I would argue, that a scientifically informed and humanistic anthropology must make a critical approach to cultural practices and values, rather as does experimental science to knowledge.

Science, as Popper has shown us, is a process whereby 'our explanatory myths become open to conscious and consistent challenge' and by which we are 'challenged to invent new myths'. Quite integral to this process is the operation of intelligent choice. As Bronowski has pointed out, when an individual proposes an hypothesis he is, in fact, making an imaginative choice; after which, his hypothesis is tested against the relevant experimental and other evidence, this evidence being allowed to decide the issue. Science is thus a value system, based on choice, for we can practise science only if we seek the truth by choosing in strict accordance with the experimental and other evidence. And so, as Jacques Monod has expressed it, 'objective knowledge cannot exist, cannot begin to exist, unless there is an active choice of values to begin with'.

This example clearly demonstrates the radical role of choice in the practice of science, which, as we all know, is an immensely potent method for obtaining accurate knowledge about the natural world. Yet science, significantly enough, is just not able, of itself, to provide us with decisive judgements about human values. Why should this be? The reason, I would suggest, is to be found in the fact that human values owe their very existence to the exercise of choice, and so are, in fact, no more than selected alternatives.

For science, obviously, all feasible alternatives are equally a part of Nature, which means that the most that science can ever do is to provide us with the fullest possible information about the characteristics and likely consequences of the alternatives between which our choices are made. And so, it is human beings, and human beings alone, who possess the capacity to choose between the alternatives which they are capable of enacting. And this means that when it comes to values, crucially important as they are in determining the ends of our actions, we have no course but to rely, finally, on our own powers of judgement, wise or foolish as they may be.

This conclusion, which is revealed by any searching analysis of the nature of the human capacity to make choices, was, in fact, reached by Aristotle in his *Magna moralia* where he contrasts science, which proceeds by 'demonstration and reason', with wisdom, which has to do with 'matters of action, in which there is choice and avoidance, and it is in our power to do or not to do'. Wisdom then, as Aristotle indicates, stems from the human capacity for alternative action, for, possessing this capacity, it becomes possible for individuals to make choices ranging from the abysmally foolish to the supremely wise, and so, wisdom is an ideal, highly appreciated in all human cultures.

One of my main conclusions then is that there is a need for a critical anthropology of human values. Human cultures being value systems are 'experiments in living', and a critical anthropology would be concerned with assessing the consequences of these 'experiments in living' in the hope that we might gradually learn to select our values with greater wisdom.

Finally, I return to the question I posed at the outset, first in the words of Margaret Mead, and then in the words of E.O. Wilson: 'What is Man's ultimate nature?' What kind of answer is to be given to this question — said by Hume to be of 'unspeakable importance' — in the light of my analysis of the anthropology of choice?

As anthropological and historical research has shown, the members of the human species are capable of a seemingly endless range of actions. Thus, as S.A. Barnett has expressed it:

> We are not, by our 'nature' obliged to adopt any particular habitat or diet; our infants can be reared in a variety of ways; and our patterns of social interaction (despite a few universal signals) are bewilderingly varied.

And even these universal signals, I would add, are open to our penchant for contrary effects that stems from choice. For example, the eyebrow flash which Eibl-Eibesfeldt describes as 'universal and stereotyped' is, nonetheless, as Eibl-Eibesfeldt himself documents, given various cultural meanings, ranging from a factual 'yes' in Samoa to a factual 'no' in modern Greece.

We here have a decisive demonstration of the way in which the human capacity for alternative action is able to modify the significance of a phylogenetically given form of behaviour. It is this same capacity that makes possible the bewildering variety of human actions, and its expression is made virtually limitless by the possession of language.

The answer that I would give then, to E.O. Wilson's question, is that humans, with their biologically given and culturally nurtured capacity for alternative action, cannot be said to have any kind of 'ultimate' nature. Indeed, I would argue that because of the way in which humans are able to create and select their own values, *Homo sapiens* can only be defined, if at all, as being, for better or for worse, a self-defining animal.

As it happens, virtually this same notion was expressed as long ago as 1793 in the answer that William Blake gave to the question: 'What is Man?' Blake's inspired answer, in his book for children, *The Gates of Paradise*, was to depict a human infant as a chrysalis, and to append the words:

> *The Sun's light when he unfolds it,*
> *Depends on the Organ that beholds it;*

so indicating that we have the invigorating potentiality, through our choices, to create our own worlds of meaning. It is to this luminous and profoundly human conclusion that the anthropology of choice leads.

CHAPTER 3

Paradigms in Collision

The Far-Reaching Controversy Over the Samoan Researches of Margaret Mead and its Significance for the Human Sciences

In September of 1983, Victor Turner, a gifted British social anthropologist who had become Professor of Anthropology in the University of Virginia, published an historic essay entitled 'Body, Brain and Culture'. I say 'historic' because it was Victor Turner's last essay, and because in it, drawing on the researches of the evolutionary neuroscientist Paul MacLean, Turner radically questioned the principal assumption that he and other anthropologists of the 20th century had been 'taught to hallow' the assumption that 'all human behavior is the result of social conditioning'.

Earlier that year, Harvard University Press had published a book of mine in which I presented a refutation of Margaret Mead's long-accepted apparent proof of this same assumption in her book of 1928, *Coming of Age in Samoa*. In it, citing the researches of MacLean and others, I argued for the adoption by anthropology and of all the human sciences of an interactionist paradigm in which both biology and culture are taken into account. Since then there has been a steadily increasing recognition of the virtues of this new paradigm, and, there are clear signs that the human sciences are undergoing a paradigm shift.

According to Marxist doctrine it is 'social existence' that determines 'human consciousness', and by the Bolsheviks of Soviet Russia it was fervently believed that under communism, human nature would radically and permanently change. By the early 1930s American observers who had visited Russia were claiming that this had already begun to happen: 'mental hygiene', it was said, was 'inherent in the social organization'.

We have now witnessed the collapse of communism, and have heard Gorbachev admit to the world at large that the experience of history has allowed the Russian people to say 'in a decisive fashion' that the Communist 'model' has 'failed'. As it had to fail, I would suppose, because of, among other things, the false assumption about human nature on which it was based.

We live in revolutionary times, and especially for those with an interest in the scientific understanding of human nature.

The assumption that 'all human behavior is the result of social conditioning' may be traced back to the eminent British philosopher John Locke. It was in an essay written in about 1660, long before there was any understanding of evolution and the brain, that John Locke, then in his late twenties, first promulgated the wholly unevolutionary doctrine that humans are born *tabula rasa*, 'empty tablets capable of receiving all sorts of imprints but have none stamped on them by nature'.

It was this doctrine, as Marvin Harris acknowledges, that at the beginning of this century became the principal assumption of the founders of cultural and social anthropology, and to be very widely accepted by the pundits of the day.

In 1915, Franz Boas's foremost student, Alfred Kroeber, had declared in the *American Anthropologist*, in attempting to establish that culture is *sui generis*, that 'heredity cannot be allowed to have acted any part in history'.

It was to make an empirical testing of this assumption that in mid-1925 Professor Franz Boas of Columbia University sent his 23-year-old student Margaret Mead to the Samoan Islands to undertake 'a study in heredity and environment based on an investigation of the phenomenon of adolescence among primitive and civilized peoples'.

The idea was that if an instance could be found that was an exception to a supposed universal phenomenon, that is the turbulence of adolescence, then this would prove that the phenomenon in question was entirely due to cultural forces.

Margaret Mead arrived on the island of Ta'ū, where her researches were to be carried out, on 9 November 1925 and left in mid-April 1926 with not more than a total of some 12 weeks having been devoted to the actual investigation of Boas's problem.

In 1928 in her *Coming of Age in Samoa*, which became the anthropological bestseller of all time, Mead concluded, in complete accord with Lockean doctrine, that 'we cannot make any explanations' of the 'disturbances' of adolescence other than in terms of the 'social environment', which, she claimed, shaped 'the individual within its bounds' in an 'absolute' way. 'Human nature' was, she declared, 'the rawest, most undifferentiated of raw material.'

These Lockean pronouncements were very much in accord with the spirit of the age. In 1930, Mead's extreme environmentalist conclusion, which had been accepted without question by Franz Boas, the venerated leader of American anthropology, was incorporated in the *Encyclopedia of the Social Sciences*, and Boas himself, in this same *Encyclopedia*, in discussing human personality, declared 'genetic element' to be 'altogether irrelevant as compared with the powerful influence of the environment'.

By the mid-1930s then, with virtually universal credence being given to Mead's Samoan researches, the notion, derived ultimately from Locke, that 'all human behavior is the result of social conditioning' had become markedly dominant in anthropology as well as in other of the social sciences.

If Mead's conclusion of 1928 had been correct it would have been the most important conclusion of 20th-century anthropology. It is now known that Mead's long-influential conclusion is wholly false. In 1983 I was able to demonstrate in detail that Mead's extreme conclusion is very definitely not supported by the relevant ethnographic evidence. And, since then, there have been even more significant developments.

It had long been a major mystery that Mead's account of Samoan sexual behaviour, on which her conclusion of 1928 rests, is radically at odds with the reports of all other ethnographers.

This mystery was solved in 1987 when Fa'apua'a Fa'amu, who is listed in *Coming of Age in Samoa* as one of her principal informants, came forward to confess that in March of 1926, as a prank, she and her friend Fofoa had completely hoaxed Margaret Mead by telling her, when she questioned them, the antithesis of the truth about Samoan sexual behaviour and values.

In Samoa the playing of such pranks, which they call *taufa'ase'e*, is commonplace. Margaret Mead had arrived in Samoa with the preconception, which she had acquired from a fellow anthropologist in Hawaii, that the Samoans, being Polynesians, were sexually promiscuous. In fact, in Samoa at that time, female virginity was very highly valued, as in their *taupou* system, and they had an exceedingly strict sexual morality. And so when Mead put to Fa'apua'a, who was herself a *taupou* or ceremonial virgin, the supposition that she was promiscuous, she and Fafoa, with sidelong glances and pinching one another, set about hoaxing her. They had no idea, says Fa'apua'a, that Margaret Mead was an author and that their wild untruths would be published as facts in an immensely influential book.

After Fa'apua'a's testimony had been carefully checked by Leulu Felisi Va'a of the National University of Samoa, detailed accounts of what transpired between Mead and her Samoan informants have been published in the *American Anthropologist* and in *Visual Anthropology Review*, both of these being publications of the American Anthropological Association, and a sworn deposition by Fa'apua'a Fa'amu has been lodged with the American Anthropological Association in Washington DC.

We are here dealing with one of the most spectacular events of the intellectual history of the 20th century. Margaret Mead, we now know, was grossly hoaxed by her Samoan informants, and Mead, in her turn, by convincing others of the 'genuineness' of her account of Samoa, completely misinformed and misled virtually the entire anthropological establishment, as well as the intelligentsia at large, including such sharp-minded sceptics as Bertrand Russell and H.L. Mencken.

That a Polynesian prank should have produced such a result in centres of higher learning throughout the Western world is deeply comic. But, behind the comedy there is a chastening reality. It is now apparent that for decade after decade in countless textbooks, and in university and college lecture rooms throughout the Western world, students were misinformed, about an issue of fundamental human importance, by professors who by placing credence in Mead's conclusion of 1928 had themselves become cognitively deluded.

Never can giggly fibs have had such far-reaching consequences in the groves of Academe.

Yet, the playing of pranks on inquisitive Europeans has long been an endearing characteristic of Polynesians. In the late 18th century, for example, when in Western Polynesia, Labillardière, a 'natural philosopher' of the French Enlightenment, set about the recording of Tongan terms for numerals. This he single-mindedly continued until he reached the improbable total of one thousand, million, million. He then communicated his findings to the Academy of Sciences in Paris, not realising that the Tongan phrases he had assiduously recorded, were, for the most part, a string of ribald obscenities.

The concept of the paradigm, as used by Thomas Kuhn in his classic essay of 1962, *The Structure of Scientific Revolutions*, refers to a ruling idea which gives rise to a coherent tradition of research. This clearly applies to the idea that 'all human behavior is the result of social conditioning' which, as Victor Turner noted in 1983, he and other anthropologists of the 20th century had been 'taught to hallow'.

It is this Lockean paradigm that, from about 1983 onwards, has been in collision with a quite different interactionist paradigm in which recognition is given to biological as well as to cultural variables.

I say 'in collision' advisedly, for the protracted controversy over my now fully vindicated refutation has revealed striking evidence of the extraordinary hold that a paradigm can have over its devotees, and of the highly emotional way in which a new paradigm, which is at odds with one of their most hallowed assumptions, is actively opposed and resisted by these devotees.

In his book of 1976 *The Selfish Gene*, Richard Dawkins coined the word *meme* to refer to any element of human cultural transmission, including ideas and beliefs. And in 1985 in *The Fabric of Mind*, Richard Bergland introduced the term *mismeme* to refer to any persistent error in the history of human thought, as, for example, Plato's mistaken notion that semen is generated in the brain, a mismeme that is illustrated in an anatomical drawing by Leonardo da Vinci, now in the Royal Library at Windsor, that dates from 1493, some 1,840 years after Plato's death in 347 BC. Some mismemes, it is evident, have a long shelf life.

In the light of our present knowledge, it is now evident that Dr Mead's ostensibly scientific conclusion in *Coming of Age in Samoa* is, in fact, a mismeme that persisted at the centre of the belief system of cultural anthropology for some 55 years.

And this means that we are afforded a rare and valuable opportunity for studying what happens when a mismeme that has become the hallowed dogma of an academic discipline is decisively disproved.

I was, of course, in writing my refutation well aware of how difficult it is to alter deeply entrenched beliefs, but I supposed, quite naively as it turned out, that if I presented sufficiently cogent evidence, it would be critically examined and, if free from error, rationally accepted.

I therefore subjected my facts to the most rigorous scrutiny and then made a special trip to Samoa to have them checked by Samoan scholars.

In 1983, soon after its publication, a Professor of Anthropology in the University of California wrote to me saying: 'the case you make "suffers" from being lucid as well as extremely powerful, so that the only responses possible are to accept it, or to confuse the issues one way or another'.

And, this poignant dilemma was greatly exacerbated by the circumstance that quite without warning my case was made known, on 31 January 1983, not only to anthropologists but to the world at large in an article on the front page of the *New York Times*, by an astute journalist, who had secured an advance copy of my book from Harvard University Press. And soon, it was on the front pages of newspapers throughout the world and on the covers of magazines like *Time, Discover* and *Life*.

In one of his essays Francis Bacon describes how, after he had slain the Sphinx, Oedipus placed its dead body on a donkey and carried it, in triumph, into Thebes. This, Bacon comments, was a 'pretty' conclusion, for 'there is nothing so subtle and abstruse, but that when it is once thoroughly understood and published to the world, even a dull wit can carry it'.

What happened in 1983 was that the body of yet another Sphinx was brought within the city walls, and a genteel silence about an intrinsically dubious anthropological supposition was broken once and for all.

Ian Jarvie, a leading philosopher of the social sciences, has argued that cultural anthropologists make up a tribe 'held together by a cult'. This cult is the cult of culture. Thus, Alfred Kroeber, in an article in *The American Mercury* in 1928, declared that 'the important thing about anthropology is not the science but an attitude of mind'.

And, this attitude of mind principally involved acceptance of the assumption that 'all human behavior is the result of social conditioning', the assumption that Mead was believed to have triumphantly validated in *Coming of Age in Samoa*.

And so, when Margaret Mead returned to New York from New Guinea in 1929, she found herself being feted as she participated in symposia with celebrities such as Havelock Ellis, Bertrand Russell and J.B. Watson, most of whom were older than her own father.

From this dreamlike beginning in the late 1920s, Margaret Mead, who was certainly a most remarkable human being, went on to become, in the words of her biographer Jane Howard, 'indisputably the most publically celebrated scientist in America'.

Fame, in Rilke's words, is 'but the sum of the misunderstandings' that cluster about a name. There is, however, as T.H. Huxley once noted, 'a tendency to idolatry in the human mind', and so Margaret Mead became, as Howard has described, 'an American ikon'.

In a leaflet of the American Museum of Natural History, she is said to have been 'the mother of *all* humanity'. And when I was in America in 1987 I came across a reference to her in *The Chicago Tribune* as having been 'earth-mother to the cosmos'.

She thus came to be viewed, during the last decades of her life, as an omniscient, wonder-working matriarch.

In the 1960s, one of the jokes then circulating in America was that when Dr Mead called on the oracle at Delphi, she addressed the age-old sibyl saying: 'Hullo there, is there anything you'd like to know?'

And, by the 1970s, she had become, in the words of a Professor of Anthropology of the University of California, 'the Mother-Goddess of American Anthropology'.

Then, in 1983, without warning and for all to witness, the Meadian reverie about Samoa was shattered. For American anthropologists, this was, as Theodore Schwartz has termed it, 'a seismic event', and, as they surveyed the fallen masonry, the embarrassment of those whose beliefs had been so rudely shaken quickly turned to fury against the antipodean antichrist who had so desecrated their *sanctum sanctorum*. And, in no time at all, as Harriot Jardine of the Denver Museum of Natural History has recorded, there were many who 'seemed willing to tear Freeman limb from limb'.

At the time, my dismemberment must have seemed a most laudable tribal project, but, as those involved should have realised, anger is a wind that blows out the lamp of the mind, and the events that followed, seen in the light of what we now know about Mead's Samoan researches, have become uproariously comic, and sadly, a demonstration that cultural anthropology as practised by some professional anthropologists is a pre-scientific ideology in which hallowed doctrine lords it over empirical realities.

Jane Howard, Mead's biographer, reports her as having told a conference of anthropologists: 'We are a family and will not have differences of opinion before strangers.'

What then was to be done about a refutation that had emanated from within the anthropological family?

It could not — as the values of science require — be accepted, or even taken seriously, for this would have been to acknowledge that the tribe had, for more than 50 years, been venerating a mismeme.

And so, infuriated by what had happened, some American anthropologists turned to rhetorically restoring the mystical aura of their totemic mother and the popular repute of her long-acclaimed *magnum opus* while, at the same time, doing everything imaginable to discredit me.

This onslaught, which began in February 1983, and was sustained over many months, was flagrantly *ad hominem*. As Lord Devlin, a British Lord Justice of Appeal, has observed: 'To discredit without proof is to smear', and the obvious object of this *ad hominem* onslaught was so to smear me with repugnant untruths as to destroy the credibility of my distressing refutation.

Anyone who seriously questions the pronouncements of a mother-goddess is obviously of unsound mind. Thus I was said to be 'crazy', to be 'fueled by accumulated venom'; to 'throw nothing but spit balls'; to have sought to bribe Samoan academics, and — most imaginatively of all — to have 'attacked a missionary with an axe'!

At first, this outpouring of spleen was a bit difficult to take. I fully realised, however, that while it was intended to intimidate and unnerve me, those who were resorting to these excesses had no arguments of any substance with which to rebut my refutation. I soon, therefore, came to regard it as both puerile and comic that such grossly *ad hominem* tactics were being resorted to by PhDs, no less, in what was already being called the greatest controversy in the history of anthropology.

1983, you will remember, was the year in which Australia won the America's Cup. Not long after this euphoric victory I received a note from a distinguished Harvard professor that read: 'The word around here is that with Freeman and the loss of the Americas Cup happening in less than a year it may be necessary to start screening visitors from Australia more carefully.'

This, at the height of the onslaught I have just been describing, amused me greatly, and in October 1983, I ended a letter to an irate female member of the American Anthropological Association, who in a massive manuscript had abused me up hill and down dale, in these words:

> Incidentally, I have been told that the American yacht 'Liberty' that was so convincingly outsailed by 'Australia II' was designed by a cultural determinist. I don't think this can be true, however, for although 'Liberty' was hulk-like at times, she was not really as bad as all that. With every good wish — to employ a selection of the epithets in your manuscript — from your simplistic, facile, odd, foolish, weak, slippery, deceptive, specious, flawed, superficial, devious, sloppy, unprofessional, naive, absurd, blatant, evasive and ridiculous colleague.
>
> Derek Freeman

It was a letter to which she never replied, though thereafter she did moderate her participation in the frightfulness of the tribal reaction to my refutation.

This frightfulness reached its apogee in Chicago in November of 1983 when, during the 82nd annual meeting of the American Anthropological Association, a special session devoted to the evaluation of my refutation, and attended by a thousand or more, was held.

The session began conventionally enough, but when the general discussion began, it degenerated into a delirium of vilification. One eye-witness has described it as 'a sort of grotesque feeding frenzy'; another wrote to me saying 'I felt I was in a room with … people ready to lynch you'.

And, at the annual business meeting of the American Anthropological Association later that day a motion denouncing my refutation as 'unscientific' was moved, put to the vote and passed.

It is to this happening that I particularly want to direct attention, because of the understanding it provides about what, following Kroeber, I shall call 'the anthropological attitude of mind'.

As well as being cultural determinists most cultural anthropologists also adhere to a related doctrine known as cultural relativism. According to this doctrine all knowledge is relative to the culture in which it is generated, and this applies even to the truth. I shall call this the tribal theory of truth.

It is this relativist anthropological attitude that gives rise to the highly unscientific notion that the scientific status of propositions can be settled by a show of hands at a tribal get-together.

In logic this is known as the *consensus gentium* fallacy. It is a fallacy that lies at the heart of the reaction to my refutation by the American Anthropological Association, a reaction, I would note, that is also a striking instance of what Irving Janis has called 'group think'. Commenting on this reaction Sir Karl Popper wrote to me as follows:

> Many sociologists, and almost all sociologists of science, believe in a relativist theory of truth. That is, truth is what the experts believe, or what the majority of the participants in a culture believe. Holding a view like this your opponents could not admit that you were right. How could you be, when all their colleagues thought like they did? In fact, they could *prove* that you were wrong simply by taking a vote at a meeting of experts. That clearly settled it. And your facts? They meant nothing if sufficiently many experts ignored them, or distorted them, or misinterpreted them.

This is a succinct account of what indeed happened, and it is now evident that the phrenetic reactions of November 1983 were desperate gestures of denial in a futile attempt to conjure me and my perturbing refutation right out of tribal consciousness.

In this the zealots in question have signally failed, for with the publication in the *American Anthropologist* and elsewhere of an authenticated account of how Margaret Mead was hoaxed by her Samoan informants, the controversy over my refutation is, in effect, over, and there are now moves afoot to rescind the motion of 1983 that so compromised the scholarly reputation of the American Anthropological Association.

As Darwin once remarked: 'It's dogged as does it', and it is indeed true that, with perseverance, the truth *will* out.

There remains, however, the perturbing phenomenon of paradigm hold: that is the way in which belief impels many individuals to cling adamantly to a paradigm which has been shown to be completely inadequate, and to attempt, as in the case of one of Mead's supporters, to defend hallowed doctrine by the outright fabrication of 'evidence'.

Garret Hardin has described beliefs as being 'silently built into the psyche so firmly that questioning them becomes quite literally unthinkable'.

And Paul MacLean, whose *magnum opus*, *The Triune Brain in Evolution*, was published in 1990, is of the view that it is our primitive limbic brain that 'provides the feeling of conviction and belief that we attach to our ideas whether they be true or false'.

This phylogenetically given propensity to believe, which is so evident in religion and politics, is something, it is important to realise, to which scientists and scholars are also prone, and which is ever liable to lead them into misconception and error.

For, while the truth is independent of belief, in that anything that is believed can be false, belief is not independent of the truth, for what is believed may be either true or false, and when it is false, it is nonetheless firmly believed to be true.

We humans then, given our evolutionary history, are fallible, language-dependent animals, peculiarly prone to the forming of misconceptions. Or, as Alexander Pope put it in his Essay of 1734: 'Sole judge of truth, in endless error hurled.'

We now know that Mead's conclusion of 1928 was in error.

Is there then, in 1991, any scientific justification for clinging, as many still do, to the Lockean doctrine that 'all human behavior is the result of social conditioning'?

The years since Boas, Mead and others proclaimed this doctrine in the late 1920s have witnessed the blossoming of evolutionary disciplines such as ethology, primatology and molecular biology, with 'the fact of evolution' during this same period having become, in the words of Stephen Jay Gould, 'as sturdy as any claim in science'.

'Light will he thrown,' Darwin wrote at the end of *The Origin of Species*, 'on the origin of man and his history,' and in 1863, in his book *Man's Place in Nature*, T.H. Huxley showed 'that no absolute structural line of demarcation … can be drawn between the animal world and ourselves'.

Scientific research during the years since the publication of Huxley's *Man's Place in Nature* has conclusively established the fact of evolution, and the fact that we humans are indeed part of the natural order.

And this being so, it is from this crucial realisation that *all* our thinking about human problems must begin. And we must, in attempting to solve them, be evolution-minded.

This realisation has been immensely strengthened by the rise of molecular biology following the discovery in 1953 by Crick and Watson of the structure of DNA.

A decade or so after this discovery, molecular geneticists began to realise that the chemicals of which plants and animals are composed might provide 'clocks' by which to measure genetic distances and to date times of evolutionary divergence. The now-flourishing *Journal of Molecular Evolution* began publication in 1971.

The principal method of measuring changes in DNA structure consists in mixing the DNA from two species and then measuring by how many degrees of temperature the melting point of the hybrid DNA is reduced below the melting point of pure DNA from a single species.

Sibley and Ahlquist of Yale University first applied this method to the taxonomy of birds, examining no fewer than 1,700 species. Then, in the 1980s, they applied this by then fully tested method to the order of primates to which we humans belong.

Their results show that humans differ from chimpanzees in only 1.6 per cent of their DNA. The remaining 98.4 per cent of our genes we share with chimpanzees. For example, our haemoglobin, the oxygen-carrying protein that gives blood its red colour, is identical in all 287 units.

This means that we are more closely related genetically to chimpanzees than are chiff-chaffs to willow warblers that differ by 2.6 per cent, yet are placed in the same genus.

There are thus, if we follow the principles of cladistics and basic taxonomy on genetic distance or time of divergence, sound grounds for including humans in the same genus with the two existing species of chimpanzee — the common chimpanzee of Tanzania and the so-called pigmy chimpanzee of Zaire — as does Jared Diamond, a Professor of Physiology in the University of California, in his book published earlier this year *The Rise and Fall of the Third Chimpanzee*, by which he means us.

Molecular biology and evolutionary genetics thus indicate that the human and chimpanzee evolutionary lines diverged as recently as six to eight million years ago, and the fact that we share 98.4 per cent of our genes with these evolutionary cousins of ours establishes that while the differences between humans and chimpanzees are conspicuous and substantial, they are not as profound as was once thought, and that as Jane Goodall concludes in her recently published account of her 30 years of research among the chimpanzees of Gombe, 'similarities in the brain and central nervous system have led to the emergence of similar intellectual abilities, sensibilities and emotions'.

What can also be said is that we humans, like our chimpanzee cousins, far from being empty tablets at birth, are born with a phylogenetically given primate nature, components of which remain with us throughout our lives beneath all of the conventional behaviours that we acquire by learning from other members of the society to which we belong.

This realisation is already having a profound effect in the behavioural sciences, as in the researches of John Bowlby and others on attachment behaviour and the primary bond. As Bowlby himself has put it: 'once we postulate the presence within the organism of an attachment behavioral system regarded as the product of evolution and having protection as its biological function, many of the puzzles that have perplexed students of human relationships are found to be solvable'.

The human genome project, which involves the efforts of hundreds of scientists around the world to 'read' the entire library of genetic information stored in the 23 pairs of human chromosomes, has been accompanied by an acceleration of research on a wide range of human conditions, such as Huntington's chorea, motor neurone disease and William's syndrome, all of which are gene-linked, and which, in varying degrees, have behavioural components. Indeed, scarcely a month passes without some new linkage being announced.

Again, since it was set up at the University of Minnesota in 1979, the Minnesota Study of Twins Reared Apart (which means that the interaction of heredity and environment can be studied in fine detail) has done research on over 100 sets of such monozygotic twins.

In a report on this research, published in *Science* in October 1990, Thomas Bouchard and his colleagues conclude that 'for almost every behavioral trait so far studied … an important fraction of the variation among people turns out to be associated with genetic variation'.

In another report published in 1990 in the *Journal of Personality*, Bouchard and McGue conclude that 'most behavioral genetic studies of personality suggest that genetic factors account for about 50% of the variance,' and that from recent research, mainly published during the 1980s and early 1990s, 'there is now a large and consistent body of evidence that supports the influence of genetic factors upon personality'.

The evidence, taken as a whole, is, they state, 'overwhelming', and so much so that 'the interesting scientific question is no longer whether or not genetic factors influence behavioral traits like personality, but rather how environmental factors combine and interact to influence behavioral differences among individuals'.

Of the fact that environmental variables are crucially important there can be no doubt. Professor Marian Diamond in her recent book *Enriching Heredity* has shown that providing an enriched environment by 'allowing rats to interact with toys in their cages produced anatomical changes in the cerebral cortex'.

While Judy Dunn and Robert Plomin, both of whom are Professors of Human Development at Pennsylvania State University, have shown in a book published in 1990 that it is differences in experiences, or in non-shared environment, that significantly account for the differences between siblings reared in the same family.

Modern research has then decisively established that heredity and environment interact to modify behaviour at every stage of development, and in the words of Robert Plomin, 'in the quantitative genetics sense that genetic effects depend upon the environment, and *vice versa*'.

This means, of course, that Mead's extreme environmentalist conclusion of 1928 cannot conceivably have been correct. And it also means that all of the human sciences, if they are to remain in touch with scientific understanding, must consign the 'empty tablets' of John Locke and Margaret Mead to the trash cans of human error, and adopt instead a fully interactionist paradigm.

On 17 July 1990 the President of the USA proclaimed the 1990s to be 'The Decade of the Brain'. This decade was, fittingly, ushered in by the publication in 1990 of Paul MacLean's epoch-making book *The Triune Brain in Evolution*. Paul MacLean has shown that the primate brain contains three basic phylogenetically given formations: the reptilian, the palaeomammalian and the neomammalian, which, both anatomically and biochemically, reflect an ancestral relationship to reptiles, early mammals and late mammals.

Our highly complex brain, in other words, is a living palimpsest of our evolutionary history. The principal feature of the palaeomammalian brain is the limbic system which is primarily concerned with visceral processes and the emotions. It is in this phylogenetically ancient part of our brains, which is virtually identical to the limbic system of our primate cousins, the chimpanzees, and which evolved long before the emergence of cultural adaptations, that our basic human nature is physiologically programmed.

Yet, even more important are the frontal lobes of our brains which have been described as 'the neocortex of the limbic system' and which as Paul MacLean and others have shown, are the seat of consciousness and of the highest human faculties, such as foresight and concern for the consequences and meaning of events, and, most importantly, of the human capacity for making choices.

As long ago as 1933, H.S. Jennings, the American microbiologist, observed that 'life is a continuous process of selecting one line of action and rejecting another', and that this applies to all animals, including one-celled organisms. And, J.Z. Young in his article on biological choice in *The Oxford Companion to the Mind* has noted that 'the continuity of life is ensured by a continuous series of selections among sets of possible alternatives', and that it is 'an essential of any living thing that it must make such repeated decisions'.

The making of choices is thus one of the crucially significant biologically given capacities of members of the human species, and so becomes a quite fundamental element in any interactionist paradigm. And, this is a conclusion, as I know from my correspondence with them, with which eminent evolutionary biologists like E.O. Wilson and Richard Dawkins are very much in agreement.

Cultural anthropologists have long claimed that it is the differences between cultures — which are often of a striking kind — that necessitate explanation in purely cultural terms. Accordingly, as by Kroeber, culture is said to be *sui generis* and uniquely human.

The researches of recent years have clearly demonstrated the inadequacy of these cultural determinist assumptions. John Tyler Bonner, of Princeton University, in his book *The Evolution of Culture in Animals*, has demonstrated the existence, in animal species other than *Homo sapiens*, of rudimentary cultural adaptations based on choice behaviour.

This particularly applies to the chimpanzee, and we are obviously dealing with an evolutionary continuity.

Noam Chomsky, as did Kroeber, has long argued that language in general and grammar in particular were the result of a sudden mutation in the human species. In a landmark study published in 1990 Drs Greenfield and Savage-Rumbaugh have demonstrated in their researches on the pigmy chimpanzee, Kanzi, that his 'capacity for grammatical rules (including arbitrary ones) … shows grammar as an area of evolutionary continuity'.

Cultural adaptations, it is now evident, are made possible by the evolutionary emergence of what Ernst Mayr has termed open programs of behaviour resulting from the gradual opening up of a genetic program to permit 'the incorporation of personally acquired information to an ever greater extent'.

And, within an open program of behaviour, a choice is made between two or more responses to produce what Bonner calls 'multiple choice behavior'.

The emergence of culture in the course of evolution is now viewed, therefore, as 'a new niche that arose from the experimentation of animals with multiple choice behavior', and it is to this evolutionary innovation that the rise of cultural adaptations in the human species is to be traced.

Furthermore, in the light of the researches of the last half-century or so, there is now no mystery regarding the primordial origin of human culture. From prehistoric archaeology and paleoanthropology we know that cultural achievements are the products of human imagination and choice, and we can trace the course of their development beyond the horizon of recorded history to a time when our ancestors had a culture little more elaborate than that of existing chimpanzee groups.

Yet, we can also be sure, in evolutionary terms, that these hominids, from whom we are descended, possessed a phylogenetically given nature, just as do chimpanzees.

From this it follows that all human cultures, past and present, are the historical creations of human populations, all of whose members possessed, as they still possess, a phylogenetically given primate nature; and further, that this primate nature, which is principally programmed in the limbic systems of their palaeomammalian brains, is ever present, in all human groups, co-existing with their cultural institutions.

It is this peculiarly human situation which accounts for the rush and turmoil of human history.

And, once this is understood, it becomes apparent that cultural adaptions can only be adequately understood with reference to the phylogenetically given human nature, from which, by the exercise of human choice, they have sprung.

Again, it is only in this context that human universals can be accounted for. As long ago as 1945, C.P. Murdock listed and discussed the 'numerous and diverse elements' that are common to all known cultures. And, in an important book published in 1991, entitled *Human Universals*, Donald Brown has demonstrated that human universals indeed exist, and that 'human biology and evolutionary psychology are the key to the understanding of these universals'.

The first international conference on human ethology was held just 14 years ago. Since then this new discipline has forged ahead and Professor Eibl-Eibesfeldt has published his monumental *Human Ethology*, which Robert Provine has described as 'a handbook of human nature'.

This it indeed is, for it demonstrates in meticulous detail an encyclopedic range of behaviours that are to be found in very many different human populations, and which, there is every reason to suppose, are species-specific.

These are empirical data that social and cultural anthropologists can no longer readily ignore.

It is also evident, from the ethological evidence, that there are not a few species-specific forms of human behaviour that ante-date the conventions of culture. And so, as John Tooby and Leda Cosmides have remarked: 'the assertion that culture explains the whole of human variation may be taken seriously when there are reports of war parties of women raiding surrounding settlements to capture men as husbands'.

In an influential paper entitled 'The impact of the concept of culture on the concept of man', first published in 1965, Clifford Geertz declared: 'there is no such thing as human nature independent of culture'. This is most certainly the case.

What can now be said in 1991 is that equally 'there is no such thing as culture independent of human nature'.

The time is thus conspicuously at hand, in all the human sciences, for a paradigm giving recognition of the radical importance of both the cultural and the biological (including choice) and of their interaction.

Instructive examples of studies conducted within such an interactionist paradigm have already begun to appear. Thus Michael Stoddart, the Professor of Zoology in the University of Tasmania, in his book *The Scented Ape*, published in 1990 by Cambridge University Press, presents an illuminating analysis of 'the biology and culture of human odour'. Professor Stoddart shows that the odours of incense that are pervasively used in cultural contexts, stimulate the human mind by unconsciously mimicking steroidal sex pheromones, just as the most preferred perfumes contain within them tiny traces of mammalian sex attractants. And so, as Professor Stoddart documents, human religious rites, in which the use of incense is so common, are accompanied by 'a basic and thoroughly animal responsiveness in their adherents, even if that responsiveness is rooted in the unconscious'.

With the realisation that all human cultures have resulted from the exercise of human imagination and choice, our biologically given capacity for making choices becomes of enormous human significance. Indeed, there are grounds for renaming our species *Homo elegans*, the choosing primate.

As the researches of Benjamin Libet have shown, conscious choice is able either to enact or to inhibit intentions that arise unconsciously, and this means that by our very nature we are, inescapably, ethical animals, for we have in the frontal lobes of our brains a mechanism for either good or evil. Further, it is our phylogenetically given capacity to make choices that makes human history, even though choice is highly determinative, largely unpredictable.

The capacity to make choices is then, as Kierkegaard once remarked, 'the most tremendous thing' that has been granted to we humans. It is tremendous in Kierkegaardian terms, in that it gives us the power to imitate either god or devil, and even to outdo either. While the chimpanzee, in Jane Goodall's words, 'is neither capable of soaring to the same heights nor sinking to the same depths'.

It is in terms then both of our primate nature and of our phylogenetically given capacity to make choices that human history must be seen, and, once it is realised that all cultures have resulted from the exercise of human choice, they are obviously open to critical evaluation, which means an end to cultural relativism. It was this that Lionel Trilling had in mind when he wrote of 'a residue of human quality beyond the reach of cultural control' that 'serves to bring culture itself under criticism and keeps it from becoming absolute'.

In a credo published when he was 80, Franz Boas gave as the principal aim of anthropology, the recognising and breaking of the shackles that tradition has laid upon us. With this I am in whole-hearted agreement. What can now be said is that this is something which any well-informed individual can achieve for herself or himself.

And it is also apparent, as J.Z. Young has noted, that democratic social systems that allow freedom of choice 'may well prove to be at an advantage over those where choice is limited by convention or compulsion'.

Within the lifetimes of most of the members of this audience there has been an historic paradigm shift in the earth sciences. It occurred in the mid-1960s with a shift from 'fixism' to 'plate tectonics'. Niles Eldredge has recorded how in undergraduate courses at Columbia University in the early 1960s, plate tectonics was said to be nonsense, while by the time he had entered graduate school, it had become the 'new truth'.

The complaint of those who so adamantly opposed plate tectonics was that they would have to forget everything they had learnt, and start all over again.

This is indeed the case when a paradigm shift occurs in human understanding, and it will also have to happen when the human sciences abandon the Lockean assumption that all human behaviour is the result of social conditioning in favour of an evolutionarily based interactionist paradigm. There will be much to learn.

As I have already noted, and as is apparent in a list of key references, which I have prepared for those who may be interested, there are clear signs that a paradigm shift is currently in progress in the behavioural and human sciences. Just when it will be complete only time will tell.

As Max Planck once remarked, new scientific realisations do not triumph by convincing their opponents, but because those opponents eventually pass away, and a new generation takes their place.

From the letters I get from young anthropologists I have every confidence in the future, and I only hope I shall live long enough to witness a revolution in anthropology as radical as that which recently occurred in the earth sciences.

For this one may indeed rationally hope, for, in the words of Bertolt Brecht, 'truth is not the child of authority but the child of time', which, like Shiva, is both a destroyer and a creator.

Let me end, then, with words based on the final sentence in Stephen Jay Gould's recent book *Wonderful Life*. We humans are, it is evident, the offspring of evolution and must establish our own paths in this most diverse and interesting of conceivable universes, which, although it is indifferent to our suffering, does offer us the boon, given to no other species, to thrive or to fail in our own chosen way.

It is then, up to us all, if we so choose, to make it a sapient way.

CHAPTER 4

'The Question of Questions'

T.H. Huxley, Evolution by Natural Selection and Buddhism

Let me begin with a brief word about the day on which I have chosen to give this talk: October the 23rd. It is a day of singular significance for skeptics like myself. It was in 1654 (when Rembrandt and Milton were alive) that Archbishop Ussher, the Primate of all Ireland, calculated that the Earth was created on 23 October 4004 BC at 9 o'clock in the morning — Greenwich Mean Time. It is now known that the Earth is about 4,112 billion years old, and that we humans, like all other living things, are the products of evolution by natural selection. Nonetheless, as I hope you will agree, October the 23rd is a poetically correct day on which to discuss T.H. Huxley's heretical 'question of questions'.

'The question of questions' for we humans, 'the problem which underlies all others, and is more deeply interesting than any other' is, T.H. Huxley declared in 1863, 'the ascertainment of the place which Man occupies in nature' and of his relation to the universe of things.

'Whence have we come' and 'to what goal are we tending': these are the questions, declared Huxley, 'which present themselves anew and with undiminished interest' to every human being born into the world.

These are indeed the great and enduring anthropological questions.

They were echoed in 1897 by Paul Gauguin in his moving painting of Polynesians (now in the Museum of Fine Arts in Boston) on which he wrote (in French): 'Where do we come from? What are we? Where are we going?' And, they were reiterated in Gustav Mahler's haunting words at the outset of this present century, 'Whence do we come? Whither does our road take us?'

T.H. Huxley's posing of what he called the 'question of questions' came at a crucial turning point in human intellectual history, just four years after the publication, in 1859, of Charles Darwin's *Origin of Species.* The answer that Huxley gave in 1863 in his book *Man's Place in Nature,* and 30 years later in his Romanes Lecture on 'Evolution and Ethics', are still of invigorating human interest.

Indeed, with the emergence in the mid-1990s of what has been called a 'new evolutionary enlightenment', Huxley's views have assumed renewed significance, and bear, with lively pertinence, on the future development of anthropology and our appreciation of what it means to be human.

It is about this 'new evolutionary enlightenment' and Huxley's concern, as an evolutionary thinker, with the human significance of choice behaviour, and of value systems like Buddhism, that I shall be speaking — values being the product of the human capacity to make choices.

Thomas Henry Huxley was born in England in 1825. After serving in HMS *Rattlesnake* for four years in Australian and New Guinea waters, as a surgeon and naturalist, and his election to the Royal Society of London, when only 26 years of age, he had by 1859 established himself as one of England's brightest young biologists.

His first reflection after mastering (in that year) the central idea of Darwin's *Origin of Species* was: 'How extremely stupid of me not to have thought of that!' In November 1859, he wrote to Darwin: 'I trust you will not allow yourself to be in any way disgusted or annoyed by the considerable abuse or misrepresentation which, unless I greatly mistake, is in store for you. Depend on it, you have earned the lasting gratitude of all thoughtful men. And, as to the curs which will bark and yelp, you must recollect that some of your friends, at any rate, are endowed with an amount of combativeness which (though you have often and justly rebuked it) may stand you in good stead. I am sharpening up my claws and beak in readiness.'

Huxley used them to telling effect during the summer of the following year when, during the annual meeting of the British Association for the Advancement of Science, he found himself on the same platform as Bishop Samuel Wilberforce.

The opposition to Darwin had indeed been fierce, and Samuel Wilberforce, the Bishop of Oxford, having assured his audience at great length that there was absolutely nothing in the idea of evolution, turned to the 35-year-old Huxley and, with smiling insolence, begged to know whether it was through his grandfather or grandmother that he claimed descent from a monkey.

Huxley slowly and deliberately arose, a slight figure, stern and pale, very quiet and grave, to tell the high and mighty Bishop of Oxford:

> I should feel it no shame to have risen from such an origin, but I should feel it a shame to have sprung from one who prostitutes the gifts of culture and eloquence in the service of prejudice and falsehood.

The effect of these uncompromising words in Victorian England in 1860 was quite tremendous: one lady fainted and had to be carried out; others in the audience jumped clear out of their seats.

Evolution by natural selection had indeed become a force to be reckoned with.

In the *Origin of Species,* Darwin had not, in fact, discussed the bearing of evolutionary theory on the human species, other than to remark that 'Light will be thrown on the origin of man and his history'.

Of all the burning questions raised by the *Origin of Species* this was by far the most unnerving.

And, having told Darwin: 'I will stop at no point as long as clear reasoning will carry me further,' it was the intellectually intrepid Huxley, who had been conducting his own research on the comparative anatomy of primates, who in London, in 1860, gave a series of six lectures on 'The Relation of Man to the Lower Animals'.

This was heady stuff, and when, in 1862, Huxley gave two lectures on this same theme to the Philosophical Institute of Edinburgh, he was accused, in a local newspaper, of blasphemy and of having committed a 'foul outrage' on the entire human species.

Huxley was not deterred. Rather, he was inclined to think it 'a good thing', as he subsequently remarked to Haeckel, 'for a man, once at any rate in his life, to perform a public war-dance against all sorts of humbug and imposture'.

In 1863, then, he published his epoch-making book *Man's Place in Nature* in which, in concise and lucid prose, he showed, as he put it, 'that no absolute structural line of demarcation … can be drawn between the animal world and ourselves'.

Huxley was thus the first to construct, on the basis of Darwin's theory of evolution by natural selection, a clear and logical image of biological man, and, as such, is clearly the founder of evolutionary anthropology.

For this achievement, Huxley was subjected, for some years, to no end of obloquy, but, as he wrote to Lord Rosebury: 'Abuse for six or seven years on the part of the public is not of the greatest consequence when one happens to be in the right and stands to one's guns.'

Scientific research during the 133 years since the first publication of *Man's Place in Nature* has demonstrated that Huxley was indeed in the right. There is now conclusive evidence of the fact of evolution by natural selection, and of the fact that we humans are part of the natural order.

Simon Easteal, who heads the Human Genetics Group in the John Curtin School of Medical Research of The Australian National University, having estimated that there is only 1.6 per cent difference between human nuclear DNA and that of chimpanzees, has, with his colleagues, concluded that humans diverged from chimpanzees only some 3.6 to 4 million years ago.

We have thus reached a juncture in the history of human understanding when, as Daniel Dennett has recently put it, 'the fundamental core of contemporary Darwinism, the theory of DNA-based reproduction and evolution is … beyond dispute among scientists'.

We are, as has become utterly clear, the products of evolution. Or, to put it more dramatically, we are not fallen angels, but risen apes. This key realisation changes all of our long-established assumptions about ourselves. In its light, human history, for the first time, becomes intelligible, and human behaviour understandable as never before. This radical transformation in human understanding — which has come to a peak in the mid-1990s — I shall call the 'new evolutionary enlightenment'. And, I confidently predict that, because it is based on fully tested scientific knowledge, it will far outshine the enlightenment of the 18th century.

But, the facing of our evolutionary origins has certain ineluctable consequences. As Stephen Jay Gould has put it, 'We may yearn for a "higher" answer — but none exists. And this explanation though superficially troubling, if not terrifying, is ultimately liberating and exhilarating.' 'We cannot,' as Gould says, 'read the meaning of life passively into the facts of nature. We must construct these answers ourselves — from our own wisdom and ethical sense. There is no other way.'

And, it is precisely here that Huxley's Romanes Lecture on 'Evolution and Ethics' becomes so important.

In March 1880, in a lecture at the Royal Institution, Huxley was able to claim that there was 'no field of biological inquiry in which the influence of Darwin's *Origin of Species* was not traceable'.

This was indeed the case. From about 1871, with the publication of Darwin's *The Descent of Man* and Tylor's *Primitive Culture,* evolution had been a dominant force in both biology and anthropology.

At this time, however, virtually all evolutionists, including Darwin, gave credence not only to evolution by means of natural selection, but also to rapid evolutionary change through the inheritance of acquired characters.

Indeed, some evolutionists, notably Herbert Spencer, were convinced that the inheritance of 'functionally produced modifications' (as Spencer called them) were the chief cause of evolutionary change in human populations.

This mistaken belief — as we now know it to be — in Lamarckian inheritance persisted unabated until just after Darwin's death, when, in 1883, August Weismann propounded his theory of 'the continuity of the substance of the germ cells'.

By the mid-1880s, Weismann's views were exciting intense interest, and, in 1887, when he attended a meeting of the British Association for the Advancement of Science in Manchester, a special symposium was arranged, devoted to the question 'Are Acquired Characters Hereditary?'

This symposium and the widespread dissemination of Weismann's ideas made the theory of the non-inheritance of acquired characters, in the words of George Romanes, the most important question that had been raised in biology 'since the promulgation of Mr Darwin's great doctrine'.

Thus, by mid-1889, Romanes ranked the widespread abandonment of Lamarckian principles that had been brought about by Weismann and others as 'a most extraordinary revolution of biological thought', and 'the turning of a tide of scientific opinion'.

It is in the historical context of this major revolution in biological understanding that Huxley's Romanes Lecture of 1893 must be seen.

With the demise of Lamarckism in the late 1880s, evolution by means of natural selection, in the eyes of many, became all-powerful.

Thus, Benjamin Kidd, in 1894, proclaimed that 'not only is the cosmic process everywhere triumphant, but our ethical and moral progress have no meaning apart from it: they are mere phases of it, developed, as every phase of life from the beginning has been, in the strictest and sternest conditions of Natural Selection' — an attitude not dissimilar to that of some contemporary sociobiologists.

It was against such deification of Natural Selection, which he had long championed as basic to the evolutionary process, as indeed it is, that Huxley recoiled in his Romanes Lecture of 1893, advancing instead an interactionist view of human action that, in the light of modern knowledge, was quite exceptionally prescient.

George Romanes was a wealthy Canadian, who, in 1892, established a fund in Oxford for an annual lecture. The first lecture was given by William Gladstone, four times Prime Minister of Great Britain and a fervent religionist, with whom Huxley had been much in controversy and of whom he did not have a very high opinion. He once compared him to 'one of those spotted dogs who runs on in front but is always turning around to see whether the carriage is coming'.

When Romanes invited him to follow Gladstone, Huxley found this so piquant as to be irresistible, and, in June 1892, he wrote to Romanes saying he had 'long been fermenting' in his head 'some relations of Ethics and Evolution' that he thought would be of interest.

This was a topic about which Huxley had been concerned ever since the publication of *Man's Place in Nature* almost 30 years previously.

Biological man, a primate among other primates, as he emerged from Huxley's *Man's Place in Nature,* raised deeply problematic questions. Much of human behaviour, it had become apparent, had to do with the fact that we human beings are indeed animals, with impulses and propensities that have evolved by means of natural selection.

Huxley was a realist with a well-informed sense of human fallibility, and, in his famous essay of 1889 on Agnosticism, he wrote:

> I know of no study which is so unutterably saddening as that of the evolution of humanity ... Out of the darkness of prehistoric ages man emerges with the marks of his lowly origin strong upon him. He is a brute, only more intelligent than the other brutes, a blind prey to impulses which as often as not lead him to destruction; a victim of endless illusions ... He attains a certain degree of physical comfort ... and then, for thousands and thousands of years, struggles with varying fortunes, attended by infinite wickedness, bloodshed and misery to maintain himself, at this point, against the greed and ambition of his fellow man ... And the best men of the best epochs are simply those who make the fewest blunders and commit the fewest sins.

For Huxley, then, the notion that evolution can provide a foundation for morals was (as he put it in 1892) an 'illusion'. It was to the human implications of this realisation that he faced up in his Romanes Lecture over which, as it was the culmination of his life's work, he took 'an immensity of trouble'.

It was delivered on 18 May 1893 in the Sheldonian Theatre of the University of Oxford, and published the following year with a Prolegomenon longer than the lecture itself.

Huxley begins his Prolegomenon by contrasting the wilderness of the Sussex Downs, the result of evolution by natural selection, with his garden there, which had been created by the exercise of human choice.

'It will be admitted,' he wrote, 'that the garden is as much a work of art, or artifice, as anything that can be mentioned' and 'the same proposition is true of all the work of man's hands, from a flint implement, to a cathedral or a chronometer,' all of which, as 'works of art, or artifice' are to be 'clearly distinguished from the products of the cosmic process, working outside man, which we call natural ...'.

Here, T.H. Huxley is making the same distinction as Karl Popper, between World 1, the world of natural objects, and World 3, the world of human creations; and, like Popper, Huxley recognises that World 3 is produced by World 2, which is the world of human consciousness and choice.

Furthermore, and most significantly, Huxley, in 1893, is recognising that what anthropologists call culture is the result of human agency or choice, this being in crucial contrast to Tylor, for whom cultures were the products of natural selection, and to Kroeber and Boas, for whom culture, like God, was *sui generis* and 'beginningless'.

Huxley then, as well as being the founder of evolutionary anthropology in his *Man's Place in Nature* of 1863, is also, in his Romanes Lecture of 1893, the founder of interactionist anthropology, which, with the eclipse of both biological and cultural determinism, is certain to become the anthropology of the 21st century.

Huxley's metaphor of the garden is one, I would note, that also applies to mental states. Thus, in discussing Candide's 'sage aphorism' that one must cultivate one's own garden, Huxley interprets the term garden broadly, applying it to 'the stony and weed-grown ground' within his own skull, as well as to 'the few perches of more promising chalk' of his garden on the Sussex Downs.

This is an age-old metaphor. In *Romeo and Juliet*, Friar Laurence, soliloquising in his cell, remarks, in words that Huxley no doubt savoured:

> *Two … opposed kings encamp them still in man as well as herbs — grace and rude will; and where the worser is predominant full soon the canker death eats up that plant.*

While in *Othello,* Iago adjures Roderigo:

> *… 'tis in ourselves that we are thus and thus. Our bodies are gardens, to which our wills are gardeners: so that if we plant nettles or sow lettuce … why, the power and corrigible authority of this lies in our wills.*

To this Shakespearean insight I shall presently return, for Buddhism, as Huxley realised, essentially has to do with the ethical cultivation of oneself by oneself. But, first I must say more about the argument of Huxley's Romanes Lecture.

Man, he argues, has worked his way to the headship of the sentient world and has become the dominant animal that he is, by virtue of his success in the struggle for existence; and, in this struggle — as among other animals — it is 'self-assertion, the unscrupulous seizing upon all that can be grasped, the tenacious holding of all that can be kept' that have mattered.

Thus, 'the cosmos works through the lower nature of man' and the cosmic process, far from being a 'school of virtue' is 'the headquarters of the enemy of ethical nature'.

For Huxley, then, 'the ethical process' is essentially in opposition to 'the cosmic process', and 'the ethical salvation of humankind consists not in imitating the cosmic process' but in combating it.

This conclusion by T.H. Huxley, the agnostic, is, most interestingly, essentially the same as that of all the great religions of *Homo sapiens,* and I would suppose that it is the evolution, by means of natural selection, of the human brain, with its limbic system and frontal lobes, that has made the devising of ethical systems an inescapable necessity.

Let me now leap forward over 90 years to a remarkable statement: 'A Sociobiological Expansion of Evolution and Ethics', which was published in 1989 by Princeton University Press, together with the original text of Huxley's lecture and an introductory essay by James Paradis, Professor of Humanities in the Massachusetts Institute of Technology, whose study of Huxley, published in 1978, is of quite exceptional merit.

The author of this sociobiological expansion of Huxley's Romanes lecture is George C. Williams, sometime Professor of Biology at the State University of New York at Stony Brook, the author of the classic book of 1966 *Adaptation and Natural Selection,* and, at 70 years of age, one of the most distinguished of living evolutionary biologists.

Williams' essay is based on his intimate knowledge of the scientific research on natural selection which has taken place over the last three or four decades, and especially since 1964, following William Hamilton's identification of the phenomenon of inclusive fitness.

In the light of his knowledge of recent research, it is Williams' view that: 'No one of Huxley's generation could have imagined the current concept of natural selection, which can honestly be described as a process of maximizing short-sighted selfishness.' 'Organic evolution,' he writes, 'is worse than traditional forms of warfare, and worse than Huxley imagined.'

> Nothing resembling the Golden Rule or any other widely preached ethical principle seems to be operating in living nature. It could scarcely be otherwise when evolution is guided by a force that maximises genetic selfishness.

And so, Williams concludes: 'Natural selection is as bad as it seems' and, as Huxley maintained, 'should, when it come to human action, be combated by ethical means'.

The sociobiological imperative, writes Williams, is thus a negative one: beware of manipulation by selfish individuals or selfish institutions, or our own selfish genes. And in this, biology can be of help in enabling us to appreciate what it is we are up against.

Towards the end of his Romanes Lecture, Huxley notes that 'the practice of that which is ethically best — what we call goodness or virtue — involves a course of conduct which, in all respects, is opposed to that which leads to success in the cosmic struggle for existence. In the place of ruthless self-assertion it demands self-restraint; in place of thrusting aside, or treading down all competitors, it requires that the individual shall not merely respect, but still help his fellows'.

And this subduing of nature to 'higher ends', this 'building up' of an artificial world within the cosmos, is, as Huxley points out, the direct result of human agency, for, to quote Huxley's own words:

> Fragile reed as he may be, man, as Pascal says, is a thinking reed. There lies within him a fund of energy operating intelligently and so far akin to that which pervades the universe, that it is competent to influence and modify the cosmic process. In virtue of his intelligence, the dwarf bends the Titan to his will.

Here, as Lloyd Morgan was quick to note, Huxley is making a crucial new distinction between natural selection and human choice as agents of change — a distinction which has recently become a major issue in behavioural biology.

I should also note, in passing, that the apparent paradox of humans, as the products of the cosmic process being nonetheless able to modify this process, is fully explained by the evolutionary emergence of the human capacity to make choices, and the realisation that this capacity is part of our biology.

One of the books that first documented the modern scientific view of evolution by means of natural selection is *The Selfish Gene* by Richard Dawkins of Oxford University. It was first published in 1976.

After discussing, in great detail, the genetic determinants of evolution by natural selection, *The Selfish Gene* ends with these two sentences that recognise a different yet pre-eminent element in human behaviour and history: 'We are built as gene machines, but we have the power to turn against our creators. We, alone on earth, can rebel against the tyranny of the selfish replicators.'

Having read these stirring sentences, back in 1977, I at once wrote to Dawkins inquiring about the remarkable power that, in his view, we humans uniquely have, and putting to him that what he was referring to is 'the human capacity to make choices'.

In his reply of May 1977, Dawkins wrote: 'I cannot disagree with you. I am referring to the human capacity to make choices.'

And, in the second edition of *The Selfish Gene* of 1989, Dawkins reiterated this recognition. 'Our brains,' he wrote, 'are separate and independent enough from our genes to rebel against them … we do so in a small way every time we use contraception. There is no reason why we should not rebel in a large way too.'

Here then, in contemporary behavioural biology, we find full acceptance of Huxley's innovative claim of 1893 that human beings by virtue of intelligence and choice can rebel against, and rise above, the titanic power of the cosmic process.

And this means, as is being increasingly recognised in the behavioural sciences, that the evolutionary emergence of the capacity to make choices — that is, of the power to select between alternatives — is of quite crucial human significance.

Indeed, it is arguably the defining characteristic of the human ethogram, being, as Kierkegaard once remarked, 'the most tremendous thing' that has been granted to humans.

In Canto 5 of the Paradiso of *The Divine Comedy*, Beatrice has this to say of humankind:

> *The greatest gift of God's largesse, when He,*
> *Created all, most prized by Him, and best,*
> *As most akin to His own quality*
> *Was the will's freedom, crown of all the rest*
> *Whence of all creatures made intelligent,*
> *They all, they only, were and are possessed.*

Here, Dante, within his pre-Darwinian world-view, is making essentially the same point as T.H. Huxley and Richard Dawkins.

However, in the light of recent evolutionary studies, it is now evident that choice behaviour — operating within the determinisms of nature — is, in contradiction of Dante, also present in infra-human animals, and is very much integral to the evolutionary process.

As long ago as 1933, H.S. Jennings, the American microbiologist, observed that 'life is a continuous process of selecting one line of action and rejecting another' and that this applied to all animals, including one-celled organisms.

William Baum, writing of animal organisms in general, has advanced as 'fundamental' the proposition that 'all behaviour constitutes choice, because in any set of environmental conditions several alternative activities can occur'.

And, John Tyler Bonner, of Princeton University, in his book of 1980, *The Evolution of Culture in Animals*, had conclusively demonstrated the existence, in species other than Man, of rudimentary cultural adaptations based on choice behaviour.

These cultural adaptations are made possible by the evolutionary emergence of what Ernest Mayr has termed 'open programs of behaviour', resulting from the gradual opening up of a genetic program to permit 'the incorporation of personally acquired information to an ever greater extent'.

An open program of behaviour is thus dependent on the brain-mediated storage and transmission of learnt, or exogenetic information, and further, does not prescribe all of the steps in a behavioural sequence, but, in Karl Poppers words, 'leaves open certain alternatives, certain choices, even though it may perhaps determine the probability or propensity of choosing one way or another'.

Within an open program of behaviour, then, a choice is made between two or more responses to produce what Bonner calls 'multiple choice behaviour'.

The emergence of culture in the course of evolution is to be viewed, therefore, as 'a new niche that arose from the experimentation of animals with multiple choice behaviour', and it is to this evolutionary innovation that the rise of cultural adaptations in the human species is to be traced.

We thus have before us, as a result of the researches of the last few decades, a view of human evolution in which the genetic and the cultural are distinct and interacting parts of a single system, and this means that, for anthropology 'the evolution of choice behavior' is the key, as E.O. Wilson put it in a letter that he sent to me in 1983.

Thus, after the publication in 1975 of *Sociobiology* in which there was no recognition of choice, E.O. Wilson's attitude radically changed, as did the attitudes of other leading biologists.

For example, J.Z. Young, formerly Professor of Anatomy at University College, London, in *The Oxford Companion to the Mind* of 1987, had this to say: 'The continuity of life is ensured by a continuous series of selections among sets of possible alternatives … It is an essential of any living thing that it must make … repeated decisions, using the best information available from outside and from within itself. And, every human being knows that this is also what he must do throughout his life.' 'Making choice,' J.Z. Young continued, 'between many nearly similar paths of action (for example, by speech) is our specifically human property' and 'we cannot be fully human unless we operate it freely'.

In 1993, Richard Passingham, of the Department of Experimental Psychology of the University of Oxford, in his book *The Frontal Lobes and Voluntary Action,* reached the conclusion that 'Human beings are capable of voluntary action in the most restrictive sense; that is, voluntary action involving the conscious comparison of alternative courses of action'.

And, Antonio Damasio, Professor of Neurology in the University of Iowa, in his book of 1994, *Descartes' Error: Emotion, Reason and the Human Brain,* has shown from his study of individuals who have suffered damage to their brains, from the surgical removal of tumours, that the human capacity to make choices is principally located in neural circuits in the frontal lobes.

The human capacity to make choices, from which both art and science spring, is thus biologically given. And further, in the light of modern research, it is evident that the two main mechanisms that have operated in the course of human evolution and history are the related mechanisms of natural selection and choice, for it is natural selection which has produced the brain in the frontal lobes of which the capacity to make choices is located.

All this, I would remark, is a validation by modern research of T.H. Huxley's recognition in his Romanes Lectures of 1893 of the key significance of the human capacity to make choices.

Yet, the freedom that our ability to make choices confers on us, is, as Dostoevsky realised, radically amoral in that it may engender evil quite as readily as virtue — evil, as in Claudius's prompting of Laertes to 'choose a sword unbated' and Laertes' choosing to anoint its point with the deadly contagion of an unction he had bought 'of a mountebank', or, on an altogether vaster and more horrific scale, the Holocaust.

And so, as Dostoevsky wrote on 9 August 1838, in a letter to his brother: 'One single condition is given to man, the weather of his soul is formed by the union of earth and heaven, and man is, therefore, a child beyond all laws … It seems to me that our universe is a purgatory inhabited by heavenly spirits imbued with evil thoughts.'

In other words, the potentiality to do good is also a potentiality to do evil, and this means that we humans, with impulses and propensities coded in our neuropeptides and in the limbic systems of our brains as the result of millions of years of evolution by means of natural selection, and possessing a freedom through imaginative choice to enact these impulses and propensities in virtually an infinity of ways, are existentially in need — as are no other animals — of a code of ethics by which to order our behaviour. We are truly the changelings of possibility.

Thus, in evolutionary terms, the emergence in human populations of the idea of an ethical god, or of some equivalent value system, is a virtual necessity.

In the Torah of the nomadic Hebrews, for example, dating from about the 13th century BC, Yahweh is depicted as setting before his chosen people alternatives of 'good' and 'evil', and then requiring of them that they should enter into a covenant with him to choose as he would have them choose.

As this historically important example indicates, virtually all human laws and rules (from wherever derived) are essentially socially preferred alternatives that have been instituted, as the jurist H.L.A. Hart has felicitously phrased it, 'with the intention of withdrawing certain kinds of conduct from the free option of the individual to do as he likes'. As Freud once remarked: 'That which no human soul desires is in no need of prohibition.'

Yet, the existence of laws by no means curbs the lawless impulses and propensities of very many individuals, for, as the French neurobiologist Jean-Pierre Changeux has put it, the limbic system and the hypothalamus have enough autonomy vis-à-vis the cortex that, under the pressure of particularly strong sensory stimulation, motivation may increase to such an extent that an individual 'goes into action' — even if the cortex says 'no' to the act in question.

And so, as Huxley noted in his Romanes Lecture, as long as our species survives on planet Earth 'every child born into the world' will bring with him or her 'the instinct of unlimited self-assertion' and 'will have to learn the lesson of self-restraint and renunciation'.

One of the conditions of the Romanes Lecture was that there should be no discussion of either religion or politics.

This imposed a peculiar difficulty on Huxley, who, having concluded that 'the proportion of good and evil in life may be very sensibly affected by human action' and having argued that so far 'as we possess a power of bettering things it is our paramount duty to use it', was in need of an example of a human value system that, while not a religion, was an example of that kind of effective combating of the cosmic process that he had in mind.

The example he chose was Buddhism, which was just becoming known in the West, mainly through the activities of Professor Rhys Davids, who in 1881 had founded the Pali Text Society, and from whose Hibbert Lectures of 1881, Huxley cited this judgement about the innovative significance of Buddhism, as enacted in the 5th century BC by the Indian moral thinker Siddhartha Gautama:

> For the first time in the history of the world, Buddhism 'proclaimed a salvation' which each individual could gain for himself or herself in this world, during this life, without any least reference to God, or to gods either great or small.

In instancing Buddhism as a humanly significant ethical system, Huxley had this to say in his Romanes Lecture of 1893:

> With just insight into human nature, Gautama declared extreme ascetic practices to be useless and indeed harmful. The appetites and passions are not to be abolished by mere mortification of the body; they must, in addition, be attacked on their own ground and conquered by steady cultivation of the mental habits which oppose them; by universal benevolence; by return of good for evil; by humility; by abstinence from evil thought; in short, by total renunciation of that self-assertion which is the essence of the cosmic process.

It is not difficult to see why Huxley, as a scientist and agnostic, was drawn to Buddhism.

On the inside of the back cover of the diary he kept as a naturalist during the cruise of HMS *Rattlesnake* in Australian and New Guinea waters, Huxley wrote, under the heading 'Thatige Skepsis' (which he got from Goethe), these words: 'An active skepticism is that which unceasingly strives to overcome itself and by well directed research to attain a kind of conditional certainty.'

And, in 1881, he declared that 'the essence of the scientific spirit is criticism'.

This, we may set beside the words of the Buddha in the *Kalama Sutra:* 'It is proper for you to doubt ... Do not go upon report ... Do not go upon tradition ... Do not go upon hearsay ...'.

Indeed, as T.L.V. Murti, in his classic study *The Central Philosophy of Buddhism*, states: 'Criticism is the deliverance of the human mind from entanglements and passions. It is freedom itself. This is the true Buddhist standpoint.'

In Buddhism, one of the five precepts (all of which are concerned with the combating of natural inclination) is 'not to lie' and the apperception of things as they actually are, or *sunyata*, is the mark of an enlightened individual.

In his famous letter to Charles Kingsley of 23 September 1860, Huxley wrote: 'truth is better than much profit. I have searched over the grounds of my belief, and if wife and child and name and fame were all to be lost to me one after the other as the penalty, still I will not lie …'.

And in this same letter of 1860, Huxley also wrote:

> The absolute justice of the system of things is as clear to me as any scientific fact. The gravitation of sin to sorrow is as certain as that of the earth to the sun, and more so — for the experimental proof of the fact is within reach of us all — nay, is before us all in our lives, if we had but eyes to see it.

This, of course, is a precise description of what Buddhists call karma: that is, the fact that in the deterministic cosmos we inhabit, we inevitably experience the consequences of our own actions and thoughts — a truth well known to poets.

Thus, Boris Pasternak writes:

> *Curling, furling,*
> *At misery's full tilt*
> *Towards me rush my own deeds*
> *Crests of past experience.*

While Milton, in his *Comus* of 1634 tells us:

> *He that has light within his own clear breast*
> *May sit i' the centre, and enjoy bright day;*
> *But he that hides a dark soul and foul thoughts*
> *Benighted walks under the midday sun*
> *Himself is his own dungeon.*

We are indeed the self-consumers of our own woes.

As we have seen, Huxley's Romanes Lecture turns on the fundamental distinction between natural selection and what Shakespeare calls the 'power and corrigible authority' of our capacity to make choices.

As Trevor Ling has documented, all Buddhist analysis begins with the recognition that humans have a measure of freedom of moral choice, and Buddhist practice has essentially to do with acquiring the freedom to choose as one ought to choose: that is, of acquiring a freedom from the passions and desires that impel us to do what we ought not to do, or not to do what we ought to do.

And to this end, the Buddhist dharma enjoins:

> *Right understanding: free from superstition and delusion*
> *Right thought: high and worthy of human intelligence*
> *Right speech: kindly and truthful*
> *Right action: peaceful and honest*
> *Right livelihood: bringing hurt or danger to no living person*
> *Right effort: in self-training and self control*
> *Right mindfulness: having an active and vigilant mind*
> *Right concentration: in deep meditation on the realities of life.*

These ethical ideals are, moreover, practical and humanly realisable ideals — as numerous Buddhists down the ages have shown.

Let me now go on to say that, like Huxley, I have drawn attention to Buddhism, not in any sense to proselytise, but to make the fundamental point that we human animals, despite having evolved by natural selection, have been able to enact ethical systems that, in the words of Ernest Gombrich, show what humans can be. And, as Gombrich comments: 'This achievement does give us all authentic and rational hope for our futures.'

What our species needs, above all else, is a generally accepted ethical system that is compatible with the scientific knowledge we now possess.

Albert Einstein thought an evolved form of Buddhism most likely to answer this need; and Huxley, I think, would have agreed.

What can be said, in the light of our present knowledge, is that it is now possible for individuals — if they so choose — to live their lives in ways that consistently generate good karma — both for themselves and for others. As Einstein remarked in one of his letters to Max Born: 'What the individual can do is to give a fine example, and to have the courage to uphold ethical values … in a society of cynics.'

This is, of course, nothing new, and I shall end with a shining example of an innovative ethical choice that would, I am sure, have appealed to T.H. Huxley. It is from *The Mahabharata,* the great epic of ancient India, whence came Buddhism.

It was Yudhisthra, the eldest of the Pandava brothers, who, you may remember, survives the slaughter of the terrible conflict with their rivals, the Kauravas.

He is finally left, burning with grief at what has happened and wandering aimlessly with his ever faithful dog.

Then, as heaven and earth reverberate, he is accosted by the sky god, Indra, and promised all the felicities of paradise if he will cast away his dog, and mount Indra's chariot.

But Yudhisthra replies: 'O lord of a thousand eyes, it is extremely difficult for one of virtuous conduct to commit an unrighteous act. I do not wish for felicity if I have to abandon a creature who is devoted to me.'

At which his dog is instantly transformed into Dharma — the personification of virtuous choice.

And, Yudhisthra, for having chosen righteously rather than to his own selfish advantage, is recognised by Indra as having no equal — not even among the gods themselves.

Such then is 'the power and corrigible authority' of our capacity for making good and wise choices, and of defining in a uniquely human way, as T.H. Huxley envisaged in his Romanes Lecture of 1893, our place in nature.

CHAPTER 5

In Praise of Heresy[1]

It is a rare privilege to be here today, and, for me, keenly nostalgic. It was just 60 years ago — in 1938, as a 21-year-old student at Victoria University College — that I first became interested in anthropology.

The late 1930s, when Hitler, Mussolini and Franco were on the rampage, were the most angst-ridden years through which I have so far lived. The mood of desperation and derring-do was caught by W.H. Auden in his poem of 1937, *Danse Macabre*.

> *It's farewell to the drawing room's mannerly cry,*
> *The professor's logical whereto and why,*
> *The frock-coated diplomats polished aplomb,*
> *Now matters are settled with gas and with bomb …*
> *For the Devil has broken parole and arisen,*
> *Has dynamited his way out of prison*
> *Like influenza he walks abroad,*
> *He stands by the bridge, he waits by the ford …*
> *Millions already have come to their harm,*
> *Succumbing like doves to his adder's charm,*
> *Hundreds of trees in the woods are unsound:*
> *I am the axe that must cut them to ground …*
> *I must take charge of the liquid fire,*
> *And storm the cities of human desire …*

The Spanish Civil War was raging. In 1937, in the Basque village of Guernica, 1,654 were killed in an air raid by bombers from Nazi Germany — a monstrous event that still lives in the torment of the painting by Picasso.

---

1   A lecture given at Victoria University of Wellington, on 2 March 1998.

When, in 1938, I participated in the Plunket Medal oratory contest of the Victoria College Debating Society, I spoke on John Cornford who had been killed in Spain on his 21st birthday. He was a Cambridge poet, and — of all things — the communist great-grandson of Charles Darwin.

Also, in those same years at Victoria, I played the part of Ernst Tausig in Clifford Odets' anti-Nazi play *Till the Day I Die,* in which there was high-flown talk of 'brothers' living in 'the soviets of the world'. It was most certainly a deeply confusing and troubled time to be at university.

At Victoria University College from 1934 I was a student of Tommy Hunter (as we called him), the Professor of Philosophy and Psychology, and of Ivan Sutherland. And then, from 1937, of Ernest Beaglehole.

After taking his PhD at London University in 1931, Ernest Beaglehole went on to Yale to work with Edward Sapir, the brilliant student of Franz Boas, who in 1899, at Columbia University in New York, had become the first professor of anthropology in America.

Boas was a German geographer, a neo-Kantian idealist with a deep antagonism to evolutionary theory, whose compelling idea, in the words of one of his students, was 'the complete moulding of every human expression — inner thought and external behavior — by social conditioning'.

It was this Boasian paradigm of the 1930s that Ernest Beaglehole adopted, having become friendly with Margaret Mead, while in America, and brought back with him to Victoria University College in 1937. To me, seeking some kind of yardstick in terms of which to comprehend human behaviour, it came as a revelation, and on 6 September 1938, in the student newspaper *Salient* (of which, at the time, I was the Literary Editor) in an article entitled 'Anatomy of Mind', I echoed Margaret Mead and Ernest Beaglehole in declaring that 'the aims and desires that determine behaviour' are all derived from 'the social environment'.

It was precisely this paradigm that Margaret Mead, in research devised and supervised by Franz Boas, had apparently validated in her famous book of 1928, *Coming of Age in Samoa.*

So taken by it was I, that in 1939, with the encouragement of Ernest Beaglehole, I decided to go to Samoa as a school teacher, so that I might investigate there at first hand the cultural determination of human behaviour. And this, without ever having completed a first degree at Victoria.

When I arrived in Samoa so complete was my acceptance of Dr Mead's Samoan writings that in my early inquiries I dismissed or ignored all evidence that ran counter to her findings. Indeed, it was not until I had become fluent in the Samoan language, had been adopted into a Samoan family and, having been given a title, had begun attending chiefly courts, that I became fully aware of the extent of the discordance between Mead's account and the realities I was regularly witnessing. When I left Samoa in November 1943, after a stay of over three and a half years, it had become apparent to me, after prolonged inquiry, that Mead's depiction of Samoa was gravely defective in numerous ways, and her account of the sexual mores of the Samoans in outright error.

By virtue of my first-hand investigations, I had — unwittingly — become a heretic.

Back in New Zealand, while waiting to sail for England as a member of the Royal New Zealand Naval Volunteer Reserve, I informed Ernest Beaglehole, as well as my other anthropological mentor, H.D. Skinner, the Director of the Otago Museum, of my misgivings about Dr Mead's account of Samoa. Neither of them took me seriously. That so famous an anthropologist as Margaret Mead could have been so mistaken was beyond belief.

This was also my experience, in the late 1940s, in the Department of Anthropology at the London School of Economics, when I reported my misgivings to Professor Raymond Firth and others. By that time Dr Mead's reputation was securely established, and Raymond Firth, as he told Mead in 1950, had 'a very real respect and admiration' for her work. And so, I remained an unrequited heretic.

The term heretic is derived from the Greek word for choice, and so refers to someone who chooses to think for himself, and then — if he has the nerve — challenges the views of those with whom he associates.

This is a hazardous and dangerous activity. In religious organisations, and especially those with creeds (a word which comes from the Latin *credo,* I believe), heresy is heavily interdicted. Heresy, then, is a word that makes those with religious beliefs shudder.

It is only a few hundred years since heretics were burned at the stake, as was Servetus in Geneva in 1553 and Bruno in Rome in 1600. And, as recently as 1993, Dr Peter Cameron, one of its ordained ministers, was convicted of heresy by the Presbyterian Church of Australia for having, in a sermon, advocated the ordination of women and questioned certain of the views of St Paul.

Religions then — Buddhism being a notable exception — are closed systems of belief, with any questioning of ordained doctrine by an adherent being strictly forbidden under pain of punishment.

In science, however, which is an open system of understanding, in which 'truth is the perpetual possibility of error', things are different. In contrast to closed systems of belief, science advances by shaking the foundations of knowledge; by showing that the relevant facts are at variance with accepted dogma.

This is a highly disturbing activity, and in the history of science has led to outright suppression, as in the case of Galileo, 'the creator of modern scientific method', who in 1633, under the threat of torture by the Holy Roman and Universal Inquisition, was forced to renounce the Copernican world system.

And although Charles Darwin finished up safe and sound in Westminster Abbey, he was subjected to all manner of obloquy after the publication in 1859 of his heretical book, *On the Origin of Species by Means of Natural Selection.*

We are here dealing with major paradigm shifts within science. The most recent of such major shifts occurred in the mid-1960s with the shift in the earth sciences from fixism to plate tectonics. Niles Eldredge has recorded how, in undergraduate courses at Columbia University in the early 1960s, plate tectonics was said to be nonsense, while by the time he entered graduate school, it had become the 'new truth'. This was with the publication in *Science* in 1966 of a key paper on the spreading of the ocean floor. Plate tectonics was the brainchild of Alfred Wegener. And, as Lawrence Bragg has recorded, when Wegener's heretical views were first presented in Manchester in 1922, the local geologists were furious. 'Words cannot describe,' says Bragg, 'their utter scorn of anything so ridiculous.'

Even in science then obscurantism can be a potent force. Indeed, as T.H. Huxley once observed: 'Every great scientific truth began as a heresy.' But because it is an open system in which (in Bronowski's words) 'the test of truth is the known factual evidence', science does genuinely advance, with plate tectonics having now surplanted fixism.

Further, as Carl Sagan pointed out in his last major book *The Demon-Haunted World,* science — remarkably — is a system of thought that actively encourages heresy, and which gives its highest commendation to those who 'convincingly disprove established beliefs'.

And so, in both science and scholarship, heretical thinking deserves to be both praised and actively practised.

But in science, being a successful heretic is far from easy, for the convincing disproof of an established belief calls for the amassing of ungainsayable evidence. In other words, in science, it is required of a heretic that he 'get it right'.

David Williamson's play *Heretic,* which some of you will have seen, is about what the great Scottish philosopher David Hume declared to be the only question of unspeakable importance: 'What is the ultimate nature of human kind?' Today, at the end of the 20th century — 60 years on from 1938 — we are, as I shall presently explain, nearer to having a scientifically informed answer to this question than ever before.

A major ideology of the 20th century — in some ways not dissimilar to Marxism — is the doctrine that 'all human behaviour is the result of social and cultural conditioning'. Under the influence of Franz Boas and his students, this paradigm, which systematically excludes biology, has dominated 20th-century anthropology. It is now commonly referred to as Boasian culturalism.

In 1917, two of Boas's students, Alfred Kroeber and Robert Lowie, without presenting any kind of empirical evidence, proclaimed that between cultural anthropology and biology there was an 'abyss', an 'eternal chasm', that could not be bridged.

It was in an attempt to obtain evidence for this ideological stance that Franz Boas in 1925 imposed on another of his students, the 23-year-old Margaret Mead, the task of studying heredity and environment in relation to adolescence among the Polynesians of Samoa. Mead arrived in American Samoa on 31 August 1925. After two months of study of the Samoan language in the port of Pago Pago, she spent just over five months in the islands of Manu'a before heading back to New York by way of Australia and the south of France.

In 1928 in her book *Coming of Age in Samoa,* which became the anthropological bestseller of all time, Mead concluded that adolescent behaviour in humans could be explained only in terms of the social environment. 'Human nature,' she declared, was 'the rawest most undifferentiated of raw material'. Then, in full accord with Franz Boas, she wrote of 'the phenomenon of social pressure and its absolute determination in shaping the individuals within its bounds'. This was cultural determinism of the most doctrinaire kind.

In 1930 Mead's extreme conclusion was incorporated in the *Encyclopedia of the Social Sciences,* and, for those who went through college in America in the 1930s, *Coming of Age in Samoa* was not only required reading but a classic of universal truths — as it was also at Victoria University College.

In 1955, after completing my doctoral studies at the University of Cambridge, and a year spent at the University of Otago, I became a member — as I still am — of the Research School of Pacific and Asian Studies (as it now is) of The Australian National University in Canberra.

And from there, in 1965 (after an encounter with Dr Mead in Canberra in 1964) I returned to Samoa for just over two years to investigate in detail every aspect of her account of Samoan behaviour.

By this time Margaret Mead had become a major celebrity. In 1969, *Time* magazine called her 'Mother of the World'. She went on to become, in the words of her biographer Jane Howard, 'indisputably the most publically celebrated scientist in America'. Indeed, during the last decade of her life, she came to be viewed as an omniscient, wonder-working matriarch. One of the jokes circulating in America at the time was that when Dr Mead called on the oracle at Delphi, she addressed the age-old sibyl with the words: 'Hullo there, is there anything you'd like to know?' In the *American Anthropologist* of 1980, she was said to have been 'truly the most famous and influential anthropologist in the world'. She had become the revered

Mother-Goddess of American cultural anthropology. A huge impact crater on the planet Venus — measuring some 175 miles across — has been named after her.

To challenge the conclusions of such a Mother-Goddess was, some would say, somewhat headstrong, but in August 1978 I wrote to Dr Mead offering to send to her a draft of the refutation of her Samoan researches, on which I was working. It was a refutation, in Popperian vein, in which I marshalled a wide range of ethnographic evidence that systematically established the extent to which Dr Mead had misreported and misconstrued Samoa. How this had happened, I had no idea. Unfortunately, Margaret Mead died on 15 November 1978, without having read my heretical text.

When it was finally published by Harvard University Press in 1983 the consternation, especially in America, was immense. Without warning, the Meadian reverie about Samoa had been shattered. For American anthropologists, as one of them remarked, this was 'a seismic event' and, as they surveyed the fallen masonry, the embarrassment of those whose beliefs had been so rudely shaken quickly turned to fury against the antipodean antichrist who had so desecrated their *sanctum sanctorum.* In no time at all, as one observer has recorded, there were many who seemed willing to tear Derek Freeman 'limb from limb'.

Anyone who challenges the pronouncements of a Mother-Goddess is obviously of unsound mind. Thus, I was said to be 'crazy', to be 'fueled by accumulated venom', 'to throw nothing but spit-balls', to have sought to bribe Samoan academics, and — most imaginatively of all — to have 'attacked a missionary with an axe'. The way of a heretic can be quite hilarious.

Things reached their apogee in November 1983 when, during the 82nd meeting of the American Anthropological Association in Chicago, a special session devoted to the evaluation of my refutation was held. It was attended by more than a thousand. The session began conventionally enough, but when the general discussion began, it degenerated into a delirium of vilification. One eye-witness has described it as 'a sort of grotesque feeding frenzy'; another wrote to me saying: 'I felt I was in a room with … people ready to lynch you'.

What is more, at the annual meeting of the American Anthropological Association later that same day, a motion denouncing my refutation as 'unscientific' was moved, *put to the vote,* and passed!

That the members of a professional association could seek to dispose of a major scientific and scholarly issue in this undisguisedly political way, attempting to dismiss by a show of hands, a refutation based on a cogent array of factual evidence is a stunning instance of the untrammelled ascendency of what Francis Bacon, in his *Novum Organum* of 1620, called 'the Idols of the Tribe'.

I now come to what was for me the most unexpected of denouements.

When I arrived back in American Samoa in 1987 I was introduced by Galea'i Poumele, the then Samoan Secretary of Samoan Affairs, to a dignified Samoan lady whom I had never previously met. During my previous visits to Manu'a she had been living in Hawaii where she had gone with her family in 1962. She was Fa'apua'a Fa'amu who, in 1926, had been Margaret Mead's closest Samoan friend. In 1987, at 86 years of age, she was still in full command of her mental faculties.

Samoans are much given to what has been called 'recreational lying', or *taufa'ase'e*. In O'Meara's words, 'all ages engage in it; people tell you stories, especially about sex, try to get you to believe in them, and then sort of chuckle inside'. Among Samoans it is 'one of their main forms of entertainment', and very much a part of Samoan culture.

Fa'apua'a's sworn testimony to Galea'i Poumele was that when Mead had insistently questioned herself and her friend Fofoa about Samoan sexual behaviour, they were embarrassed, and — *as a prank* — had told her the exact reverse of the truth.

In 1988, and again in 1993 (after I had found in the Library of Congress a number of letters, all of them in Samoan, that Fa'apua'a had written to Mead in 1926), Fa'apua'a's testimony was investigated in great detail by Dr Unasa L. Va'a (as he now is) of the National University of Samoa. In 1990, I obtained from the archives of the American Philosophical Society, in Philadelphia, copies of the personal correspondence of Franz Boas and Margaret Mead for the years 1925 and 1926. Then, in 1992, in Washington DC I was able to research all of Mead's Samoan papers in the Manuscript Room of the Library of Congress. From these and other primary source materials it has been possible to determine just what befell the 24-year-old Margaret Mead in Samoa in 1926. It is a revealing story.

When Margaret Mead was Boas's PhD student at Columbia her fervent desire was to do ethnological research in some untouched part of Polynesia. And so, when Boas imposed on her his quite different project in which she had no real interest, she at once entered into a private arrangement with the Bishop Museum of Honolulu to do in Samoa the kind of ethnological research on which her heart was set. This arrangement she kept entirely secret from Boas, her official supervisor, who had repeatedly instructed her to refrain from ethnological research while in Samoa. Immensely ambitious, she was defiantly burning her candle at both ends. It was to lead directly to her hoaxing by Fa'apua'a and Fofoa.

On New Year's Day 1926, the island on which Mead was working was stricken by a devastating hurricane, which, in Mead's words, 'razed 75% of the houses of Ta'u to the ground' and 'generally disorganized native society'. Largely because of this disruption, Mead persisted in her ethnological research for the Bishop Museum, postponing indefinitely any systematic investigation of the sexual behaviour of the adolescent girls she was supposed to be studying.

So it was, during the ides of March, while doing ethnology on the island of Ofu, and with her work on adolescents, through neglect, being in a state of acute crisis, that Mead, hoping to make up for lost time, began questioning her travelling companions Fa'apua'a and Fofoa (who were both 24 years of age) about the sexual behaviour of Samoan girls.

From Mead's diary and from Fa'apua'a's testimony we can date this questioning to 13 March 1926. What the embarrassed Fa'apua'a and Fofoa told Mead was the exact reverse of the truth, and we have the clearest possible evidence of this in a letter that Mead wrote to Boas the very next day. In it she tells Boas that in Samoa there is no 'curb' on sexual behaviour during adolescence, this being precisely the false information which, as a prank, had been communicated to her the previous day by Fa'apua'a and Fofoa. In fact, in Samoa in those days there was a virginity cult with ritual defloration at marriage. And so, Mead's letter to Boas of 14 March 1926 is, for the historian, 'a smoking gun', and proof positive that she had indeed been hoaxed.

A few days after her hoaxing Mead wrote to Boas again saying she was proposing to cut short her fieldwork by over a month. Her planned investigation of the sexual behaviour of the adolescent girls she was supposed to be studying was never undertaken. Instead, she relied on the totally false information with which she had been hoaxed.

And so, as David Williamson has me saying in his play: 'A whole view of the human species was constructed out of the innocent lies of two young women.'

We are here dealing with one of the most remarkable happenings in the intellectual history of the 20th century. Margaret Mead, the historical evidence demonstrates, was comprehensively hoaxed by her Samoan informants. Then in her turn, by convincing Franz Boas, Bronislaw Malinowski, Ruth Benedict and others of the 'genuineness' of her account of Samoa, she unwittingly misinformed and misled the entire anthropological establishment, as well as the intelligentsia at large, including such sharp-minded skeptics as Bertrand Russell and H.L. Mencken.

That a Polynesian prank should have produced such a result in centres of higher learning throughout the Western world is surpassingly comic. But behind the comedy there is a chastening reality. It is now apparent that for decade after decade in university and college lecture rooms throughout the Western world, students were misinformed about an issue of fundamental importance by professors, who, by placing credence in Mead's conclusion of 1928, had themselves become cognitively deluded.

All in all, it is one of the most momentous stories in the history of anthropology. It is told, in detail, in my forthcoming book *The Fateful Hoaxing of Margaret Mead: An Historical Analysis of Her Samoan Researches*, which is to be published later this year in the USA by Westview Press.

The aim of both Boas and Mead was to exclude biology — and particularly evolutionary biology — from the study of human behaviour. Although, as is now known, Mead's extreme conclusion in *Coming of Age in Samoa* was counterfeit and wholly misleading, it was enthusiastically accepted by Franz Boas. In 1934, when still Professor of Anthropology at Columbia University, Boas concluded in the *Encyclopedia of the Social Sciences* that 'the genetic elements which may determine personality' are 'altogether irrelevant as compared with the powerful influence of the cultural environment'. It is this anti-evolutionary ideology that has dominated thinking in the social sciences for most of the 20th century.

We now know that Mead and Boas were massively mistaken. Boas died in 1942. By that time Oswald Avery and his colleagues were already actively exploring the characteristics of DNA, which had been discovered as long ago as 1869. Since the determination of the chemical structure of DNA by Crick and Watson in 1953, an event ranked by John Maynard Smith as 'the most important discovery in biology since Darwin', genetics and molecular biology have effloresced in the most prodigious way. 'We have witnessed,' in the words of Ernst Mayr, 'unprecedented breakthroughs in genetics, cellular biology and neuroscience …'. Never before have there been such fundamental advances in our understanding of the mechanisms of life.

In a recent paper on 'The Human Genome' by Mandel, it is estimated that there are 'about 3,000 genetic diseases' known in humans, with many of them 'affecting brain function' or behaviour in some way. This makes nonsense of Boas's conclusion of 1934.

From the work on the human genome, as on the genomes of other forms of life, it has become apparent, as the great evolutionary biologist Dobzhansky once remarked, that we humans are 'kin to everything that lives'. A remarkable instance of this has recently come to light with the successful sequencing of the 6,000 or so genes of yeast — a unicellular fungus that is used in the baking and brewing industries. Howard Bussey of McGill University, who coordinated the sequencing of yeast chromosomes 1 and 16, was giving a seminar on his work when a distinguished colleague raised his hand. 'What,' he asked, 'is a muscle protein like myosin doing in yeast? Yeast doesn't move!' 'Myosin,' Howard Bussey explained, 'does the same job in yeast as it does in people. It binds with actin and other proteins that move things like mitochondria around in cells.' 'The contractile proteins, as in yeast,' Bussey went on, 'or, for that matter in tomatoes, are woven together in animals to form muscles.' Something to reflect on when next you have a tomato sandwich: we are indeed kin to everything that lives.

Simon Easteal, who heads the Human Genetics Group in the John Curtin School of Medical Research at The Australian National University, having established that there is only 1.6 per cent difference between human nuclear DNA and that of chimpanzees, has, with his colleagues, concluded that humans diverged from chimpanzees only some 3.6 to 4 million years ago. Other geneticists suppose it to have been up to 5 million years ago.

We have, then, reached a juncture in human understanding when, as Daniel Dennett has recently put it: 'the fundamental core of contemporary Darwinism, the theory of DNA-based reproduction and evolution, is … beyond dispute among scientists'.

We are, it is now utterly clear, the products of evolution. Or, to put it more dramatically, we are not fallen angels but risen apes. This key realisation changes all of our long-established assumptions about ourselves. In its light, human history, for the first time, becomes fully intelligible, and human behaviour understandable as never before. This radical transformation in human understanding — which has come to a peak in the late 1990s — I shall call 'the new evolutionary enlightenment'. And, I confidently predict that, because it is based on fully tested scientific knowledge, it will ultimately far outshine the enlightenment of the 18th century.

The fundamental advances of the last 40 years in genetics and molecular biology have been accompanied by comparable advances in primatology, human ethology and, in particular, in the neurosciences. On 17 July 1990, the President of the United States of America proclaimed the 1990s to be 'The Decade of the Brain'. It was ushered in by the publication of Paul MacLean's book *The Triune Brain in Evolution,* in which it is shown that the human brain contains three phylogenetically given formations, the reptilian, the palaeomammalian, and the neomammalian, which reflect an ancestral relationship to reptiles, early mammals and late mammals.

The principal feature of the palaeomammalian brain is the limbic system which is primarily concerned with visceral processes and the emotions. It is in this phylogenetically ancient part of our brains, which is virtually identical with the limbic systems of our primate cousins, the chimpanzees, and which evolved long before the emergence of cultural adaptations, that much of our human nature is physiologically programmed.

Thus, Joseph LeDoux and his colleagues have recently shown that the amygdala (which is part of what MacLean calls the limbic system) has to do, in all species that have an amygdala, with fear responses. 'The remarkable fact,' states LeDoux, 'is that at the level of behavior, defence against danger, is achieved in many different ways in different species, yet the amygdala's role is constant, and has been maintained through diverse branches of evolutionary development.' The amygdala then is one of the 'emotion systems' of the human brain, each of which, as LeDoux puts it, 'evolved for a different functional purpose and each of which gives rise to different kinds of emotions'. Further, 'these systems operate outside of consciousness and constitute the emotional unconscious'.

The amygdala in *Homo sapiens* is thus in no sense the product of recent social or cultural conditioning. These findings make arcane nonsense of the claim of Clifford Geertz, following Boas and Mead, that 'our emotions … like our nervous system itself' are 'cultural products'. Rather, as Roger Shepard notes in his contribution to the recently published *Characterizing Human Psychological Adaptations,* certain elements of human cognition and behaviour are phylogenetically given. As W.D. Hamilton has precisely put it, 'the *tabula* of human nature was never *rasa* and is now being read'.

Even more significant are the frontal lobes of our brains, often described as 'the neocortex of the limbic system', which are the seat of consciousness and, most importantly, of the human capacity to make choices. This capacity, as the researches of J.Z. Young, John Tyler Bonner, Antonio Damasio and others have demonstrated, is *biologically* given. Thus, as Richard Passingham, one of the foremost researchers in this field, has put it: 'Human beings are capable of voluntary action in the most restrictive sense; that is, voluntary action involving the conscious comparison of alternative courses of action.'

The human capacity to make choices, from which both art and science spring, is then biologically given. And further, in the light of modern research, it is evident that the two main mechanisms that have operated in the course of human evolution and history are the related mechanisms of natural selection and choice, for it was natural selection that produced the brain in the frontal lobes of which the capacity to make choices is located.

Our biologically given capacity for choice is then of enormous human significance. For one thing, it means that, by our very nature, we are inescapably ethical animals, for we have in the frontal lobes of our brains a mechanism for either good or evil.

Further, as R.J. Rose has recently put it: 'We inherit dispositions not destinies. Life outcomes are consequences of lifetimes of behavior choices. The choices are guided by our dispositional tendencies, and the tendencies find expression within environmental opportunities that we actively create.' Thus, as McGue and Bouchard have remarked: 'The heritability of psychological function does not imply the genetic determination of human behavior.' Indeed, there are good grounds for renaming our species *Homo elegans* — the choosing primate.

In 1965, Clifford Geertz defiantly declared: 'there is no such thing as human nature independent of culture'. This is most certainly true. What can be said at the end of the 20th century is that it is equally true that 'there is no such thing as culture independent of human nature'.

It was Margaret Mead's view that anthropology will evolve into 'an increasingly exact science'. It is now evident that the way in which this is likely to be achieved is by the emergence of a new anthropological paradigm in which full recognition is given to both biological and cultural variables, and to their complex interaction.

As long ago as 1987, in an editorial in *Science,* Daniel Koshland declared: 'the debate on nature and nurture in regard to behavior is basically over. Both are involved, and we are going to have to live with the complexity.' This is unquestionably the case, and at the end of the 20th century it is crystal clear that anthropology, of necessity, must operate within an interactionist paradigm. And this, ineluctably, involves the abandonment of Boasian culturalism, which is now a completely superseded belief system. In adolescent, as in *all* human behaviour, *both* 'physiological conditions' and 'cultural conditions' (to use Boas's terms) are always involved, in varying degree: it is *never* 'nature or nurture' but always 'nature and nurture'.

The time is thus conspicuously at hand for an anthropological paradigm that gives full recognition to the radical importance of both biological and cultural variables, and of their past and ongoing interaction. To enact this — as I say in the Afterword to *The Fateful Hoaxing of Margaret Mead* — is the principal task of the anthropology of the 21st century.

In the *New Zealand Free Lance* of 12 January 1938, there was a full page of photographs on a 'Climbing Tragedy in the Southern Alps'. It recorded how Norman Dowling, aged 26, of Wellington had slipped on a precipitous slope of Mr Evans and fallen to his death, dragging his two companions with him. Aged 21, I was one of those companions. If I had been killed, it is unlikely in the extreme that the Mead myth about Samoa would ever have been exposed. Such are the vicissitudes of human history.

In the 1938 issue of *Spike,* the literary journal of Victoria University College, there is a poem of mine: 'for a friend killed on Mt Evans'. It contains two lines that will serve as an epitaph for all headstrong and dogged heretics. With these lines then — of 60 years ago — I end this wittingly nostalgic lecture:

> *Grant vision's end, to apprehend*
> *All substance and illusion.*

> *E fili e le tai aga a le va'a*
> The qualities of a canoe are tested in deep waters
> (Samoan proverb)

CHAPTER 6

Margaret Mead's *Coming of Age in Samoa* and Boasian Culturism

An Historical Analysis

In 1925, Franz Boas, 'the father of American anthropology', faced by what he called 'the difficulty of telling what part of our behavior is socially determined and what is generally human', arranged for his 23-year-old student Margaret Mead to go to Samoa in Western Polynesia. 'The compelling idea' of Franz Boas's 'life work' was (according to his student Leslie Spier) 'the complete molding of every human expression — inner thought and external behavior — by social conditioning'. Mead's task was to obtain, under the direction of Franz Boas, an answer to 'the problem of which phenomena of adolescence are culturally and which physiologically determined'. In 1928, in *Coming of Age in Samoa,* Mead concluded unreservedly that the phenomena of adolescence could only be explained in terms of 'the social environment'.

Meads extreme conclusion was very much to Boas's liking, and early in the 1930s he asserted, in the *Encyclopedia of the Social Sciences* that 'the genetic elements which may determine personality' are 'altogether irrelevant as compared with the powerful influence of the cultural environment'. This is a succinct statement of the Boasian culturalism that 'from the late 1920s' became, in the words of George Stocking, the leading historian of American anthropology, 'fundamental to all of American social science'. In this way, Margaret Mead's *Coming of Age in Samoa,* with its approving foreword by Franz Boas, became one of the most influential anthropological texts of the 20th century. It is this situation that makes the historical study of what happened to the young Margaret Mead in Samoa so fundamentally important. We are dealing, I would emphasise, with a strictly historical problem. What I want to do is to give a brief and final account of the historical research that I have over many years been conducting into Margaret Mead's Samoan fieldwork of 1925–1926.

My book of 1983, *Margaret Mead and Samoa: The Making and Unmaking of an Anthropological Myth,* contained a detailed refutation of Mead's general conclusion of 1928 and, in particular, of the account of the sexual mores of the Samoans on which her general conclusion was based. So highly inaccurate was Mead's account (as Eleanor Gerber reported in 1975) that many Samoans believed that her 'informants must have been telling her lies in order to tease her'. In 1983, however, there was a complete lack of corroborative evidence for this Samoan belief. Then, in 1987, while visiting American Samoa, I was introduced, by the late Galea'i Poumele, a high chief of Fitiuta and the then secretary of Samoan affairs of the government of American Samoa, to Fa'apua'a Fa'amu, who, in 1926, had been Mead's closest Samoan friend. She had just returned to her natal island of Ta'u after having lived since the early 1960s in Hawaii. According to Fa'apua'a Fa'amu's sworn testimony to Galea'i Poumele, which was recorded on video on 13 November 1987, she and her friend Fofoa (who died in 1936) had, during the course of travelling with her in March of 1926 on the island of Ofu, comprehensively hoaxed Margaret Mead about the sexual mores of the Samoans.

There was thus, from 1987, a conspicuous need to test the sworn evidence of Fa'apua'a Fa'amu against the circumstances of Mead's Samoan fieldwork. A meticulous examination of all of the available primary sources was required. For the conscientious historian, the point had been reached where there could be no avoiding this question: '*What, in fact, actually happened during Margaret Mead's brief sojourn in the remote islands of Manu'a in the mid-1920s?*'

The first step was to arrange for Fa'apua'a Fa'amu to be questioned in much greater detail than had been possible in November of 1987. Accordingly a series of questions based on all of the then available information on Mead's Samoan fieldwork was drawn up and arrangements were made for the Samoan *ali'i,* Unasa, Dr L.F. Va'a, who was studying for a doctorate in anthropology from The Australian National University, and who, in 1988, was a lecturer in Samoan language and culture at the National University of Samoa, to travel to Fitiuta to interview Fa'apua'a. On 2 May 1988,

Unasa interviewed Fa'apua'a Fa'amu for a total of six hours and put to her over 250 questions dealing with her life history and with numerous aspects of her relationship with Margaret Mead during the first three months of 1926. Most of these questions had been prepared in advance on the basis of what was already known from published sources. Fa'apua'a's statements were recorded verbatim in Samoan. They provided a mass of detailed information of relevance to Mead's activities in Manu'a during 1926. A preliminary account of this research — entitled 'Fa'apua'a Fa'amu and Margaret Mead' — was published in the *American Anthropologist* in December 1989.

In 1990, when I was a Woodsworth visiting scholar at the Institute of the Humanities at Simon Fraser University, British Columbia, the late Professor Douglas Cole presented me with photocopies of the correspondence of 1925–1926 between Franz Boas and Margaret Mead which he had obtained from the American Philosophical Society during his own research on the biography of Franz Boas. It was after studying this correspondence that I decided to embark on the historical study both of Margaret Mead's years as a student of Franz Boas and of the fieldwork she undertook in Samoa under his supervision. My first approach was to the archivist of the National Academy of Sciences, who sent me, in July 1991, a copy of Mead's 'roster file' for the years 1925–1926 from the archives of the National Research Council of the USA. Then, in 1992 I travelled to Washington DC to study, in the Manuscript Room of the Library of Congress, all of Margaret Mead's Samoan papers.

In 1989, after the testimony of Fa'apua'a Fa'amu had become known, the historian George Stocking expressed skepticism about 'octogenarian recollections' of 'events of sixty years before'. It was therefore decided to check Fa'apua'a's recollections of the time she spent with Margaret Mead in further detail against independently established historical facts that I had obtained from Mead's Samoan papers in the Library of Congress. Arrangements were made for Unasa L.F. Va'a (who was in Samoa conducting his own research for his dissertation in anthropology at The Australian National University) to revisit Fitiuta with a further series of questions based on Mead's Samoan papers of 1925–1926. This further research produced quite definite evidence that Fa'apua'a in 1993, as in 1988, had substantially accurate memories of Manu'a in 1926, including the time that she and Fofoa had spent with Mead on the islands of Ofu and Olosega on March of that year. On 3 May 1993, for a second time,

Fa'apua'a swore on the Bible before witnesses that all of the testimony she had given to Unasa L.F. Va'a was to the best of her knowledge 'true and correct in every way'.

During the 1990s additional evidence was sought from various other sources, right up to the time of the crucially significant discovery in 1999 of Mead's account (published in New York in 1931) of what had transpired between Fa'apua'a and Fofoa and herself on the island of Ofu in March of 1926. The historical analysis that follows is thus based on all of the available primary sources.

The vitally significant information for the understanding of what happened to Margaret Mead in March of 1926 is the fact that she brought with her to Samoa in 1925 a fundamentally mistaken preconception about the sexual mores of the Samoans she was about to study. This key historical fact is documented in Mead's own papers. It was a preconception she had formed from 1924 onwards about Polynesian sexual behaviour from her reading of the literature on Tahiti and the Marquesas. It had been further fed in the instruction she received at the Bishop Museum in Honolulu in August 1925 from Edward Craighill Handy. Although neither Edward Craighill Handy nor Margaret Mead realised this, the sexual mores of Samoa were markedly different from those of either Tahiti or the Marquesas.

Mead was given first-hand information about this marked difference on 10 October 1925, when she travelled to Leone on the island of Tutuila to interview Helen Ripley Wilson, a part-Samoan who spoke English and, according to Mead, was 'a Samoan by sympathy' and 'thoroughly conversant with Samoan custom'. Mead had gone to Leone especially to question Helen Wilson about the Samoan *taupou* system and the position of girls and women in Samoan society.

In Samoa, an *ali'i*, or titular chief of high rank, has the right to confer on one of the sexually mature virginal girls of his family the rank of *taupou*, the girl chosen being usually one of his own daughters. In a Samoan family, daughters possess a special status of respect vis-à-vis their brothers, and so a *taupou* is the apotheosis of the honorific standing of a chiefly family, with her hand in marriage being much sought after by other titular chiefs of rank. A *taupou*, like an *ali'i*, has an accompanying title unique to the family of which she is a member, and she is given a ceremonial installation in which all members of the community participate. *Taupou* were to be found in every village in which there were titular chiefs of rank, and their traditional titles were known and respected throughout Samoa.

Mead had taken with her to Leone a list of 25 typewritten 'Questions to ask Mrs. Wilson'. She was correctly informed by Helen Wilson that only *ali'i* had the 'right to have a *taupou*'. A *taupou*, however, belonged to the whole village. As a virgin, the *taupou* was chaperoned even within her own village, by the wife of a talking chief, or *tulafale*, and if she went to another village, her 'chaperone' had to go with her. Indeed, as Mead recorded in her fieldnotes, 'girls even of common families' are 'never sent from village to village singly, without an older woman'. Further, 'It was not considered right to send a girl when there were plenty of men around the place.' Here, Mead was being accurately informed about the way in which every attempt is made in Samoa to safeguard the virginity not only of the *taupou* but also of the girls of 'common families'. This safeguarding of virginity in the traditional society of Samoa was to ensure that a male, and particularly a male of rank, could be certain that the female he was marrying was a *virgo intacta* who had not been possessed by any other male, this being regarded as imperative for the maintenance of masculine honour and prestige. Furthermore, this safeguarding of nubile females was associated with the distinctively Samoan custom of the formal testing of virginity at marriage by the manual defloration of the 'bride' before witnesses, by a male representative of the 'bridegroom'.

On 9 November 1925, about a month after she had interviewed Helen Wilson in Leone, Margaret Mead took up residence in the US Naval Dispensary on the island of Ta'u in Manu'a. Rather than live with a Samoan family she had decided to live with expatriate Americans, and the US Naval Dispensary remained her research headquarters for the five months that she spent in Manu'a. In this way Mead chose to cut herself off from the realities of Samoan existence.

In her letter of 29 November 1925, she told Boas that 'any discussion of sex and religious matters' would have to wait until she had obtained 'greater linguistic practice'. On 16 December 1925, however, Mead interviewed To'aga, the English-speaking wife of Sotoa, the high chief of Luma, about both female virginity and marriage in Manu'a. She was told, as is recorded in her fieldnotes, that 'virgins formerly left their hair long on top and shaved at the sides' and that 'if a girl eloped or became pregnant her head was shaved that all might know of her disgrace'. To'aga then went on to inform Mead that at the marriage of a *taupou* or ceremonial virgin, 'the tokens of virginity were taken by the boy's *tulafale* (or talking chief), while in the marriage of an ordinary girl the ceremony takes place in the house, where only the family and the boy's friends are present and some elderly man, chosen by the boy, performs the ceremony'. This account, it will be noted, is very much in accord with what Helen Wilson had told Mead in Leone on 10 October 1925 about the sexual mores of the Samoans.

In her report to the National Research Council of the USA of 6 January 1926, Mead correctly reports (as she had been told by To'aga) that, in the case of a *taupou*, and also at the marriage of a girl of lesser rank, 'a representative of the bridegroom is permitted to test the virginity of the bride'. This is an accurate account (as far as it goes) of the traditional sexual mores of the Samoans. But then, in this same report, and despite the fact that she had engaged in no direct investigation of the sexual behaviour of adolescent girls, Mead adds the completely contradictory and entirely false information that in Manu'a there was 'an extensive tolerance of premarital sexual relations'. This then is the preconception that Mead had brought with her to Samoa.

Margaret Mead's passionate desire as a 23-year-old student at Columbia University was to undertake ethnological research in the remote Tuamotu Islands of Polynesia. To this Boas would not agree, considering it to be too hazardous. Instead, he imposed on his 23-year-old student a study of his own devising: 'to see how much adolescent behavior is physiologically determined and how much it is culturally determined'. It was agreed that this study would take place in American Samoa which was in regular communication with the USA. As Mead herself has stated, she was 'explicitly instructed by Professor Boas to resist the temptation to do standard ethnography'.

However, during her visit to the Bishop Museum in Honolulu, en route to Samoa, the Museum's Director, Herbert P. Gregory, offered to publish, as one of the prestigious Bulletins of the Bishop Museum, any account of the ethnology of Samoa that she might be able to complete. The temptation was too strong, and on 1 November 1925, some days before she had even arrived there, Mead wrote to Edward Craighill Handy, agreeing to work on an 'Ethnology of Manu'a' for the Bishop Museum. Mead's fieldwork in Manu'a was planned to last for six months, a quite limited period for the completion of the task that Boas had imposed upon her. Yet from the time of her first arrival in Manu'a, in direct defiance of the instruction she had been given by Boas, Mead gave as much as one third of her time to ethnological research for the Bishop Museum.

During December 1925, in addition to this ethnological research, Mead completed a 'detailed census of the 856 inhabitants and the one hundred households of the villages of Luma, Si'ufaga and Faleasao', in which all of the girls she was proposing to study lived. However, at the time of her report of 6 January 1926 to the National Research Council of the USA, she had made no systematic study of the sexual behaviour of the adolescent girls of Manu'a.

On 1 January 1926, the island of Ta'u was struck by a devastating hurricane. It 'destroyed every house' in a nearby village and seriously disrupted for some three weeks the research on adolescent girls that Mead was waiting to begin. When she wrote to Boas on 16 January 1926 she was in a distraught state. She had, she said, 'no idea' whether she was 'doing the right thing or not' or 'how valuable' her 'results' would be. It all weighed 'rather heavily' on her mind. 'Will you,' she asked her supervisor, 'be dreadfully disappointed in me?' And her letter ended with the agitated words: 'Oh I hope I won't disappoint you in this year's work.'

On 19 January 1925, Mead made her first dated entry in the loose-leaf folder in which she recorded her notes on the sexual behaviour of adolescent girls. The dated notes in this loose-leaf folder continue until 15 February 1926. They comprise some 50 pages, each measuring 7½ by 5 inches. The notes themselves are highly unsystematic, fragmentary and anecdotal. Furthermore they provide abundant evidence that, because Samoan girls were, as Mead says of one of them, 'very secretive', she was having extreme difficulty in collecting any kind of reliable information.

Ordinarily, most of the girls Mead had selected for study were at school and 'inaccessible except for about two hours a day'. This situation had changed when the school closed after the hurricane of 1 January 1926. It was to reopen on 1 March 1926. The final fortnight of February 1926 was thus the last chance that Mead had for concentrated research on her adolescent girls. Yet when the opportunity arose, with the arrival of an expedition from the Bishop Museum, she completely abandoned further research on these girls and travelled on 20 February 1926 to Fitiuta at the eastern end of the island of Ta'u, there to engage until 3 March 1926 in ethnological research.

It so happened that Andrew Napoleone, the Samoan school teacher in Fitiuta, spoke excellent English, and in 36 pages of her field notebook number 4, Mead recorded the statements of Napoleone about the sexual mores of the Samoans. Chapter 10 of *Samoa: Yesterday, Today and Tomorrow,* by Napoleone A. Tuiteleapaga, which Mead, in her introduction, describes as 'a treasury of astute comments on Samoan custom and culture', is entitled 'The Role of the Woman'. In it Napoleone states (on p.431) of all Samoan girls:

> After she has reached puberty, her girlhood and womanhood periods are guarded very closely; everywhere she goes she is escorted by her mother, older married sisters, or the family of old ladies. Her brothers, because of the brother–sister taboo, would not dare to go near her, but kept an alert ear-eye watch to assure her safety, so that she can keep her virginity until she gets married.

Again, on page 63 of his chapter on marriage, Napoleone writes: 'Brothers and other male relatives did everything to protect their virgin female relatives. As a result of this custom, women up to the age of twenty-five years kept their virginity to the time of their marriage, hence the custom of *fa'amasei'au* (defloration of the virgin bride).'

It was to this custom that prime attention was given in the information that Andrew Napoleone gave to Mead, at her request, when they conversed in Fitiuta in February 1926. Thus Mead's notebook number 4 begins with Napoleone's account of ritual defloration at marriage. In this ritual, as Mead's own notes of February 1926 record, the talking chief of the bridegroom, having wrapped his first and second fingers in a piece of white bark cloth or, if that was unavailable, white trade cloth, would rupture the bride's hymen. The cloth stained with hymenal blood was then, with a great shout, held up 'for all to see'. When it was known that the bride was a virgin, drums were beaten, objects broken, guns fired, and there was feasting. If a girl was not a virgin, so Napoleone stated, it was for her to confess this in advance to the officiating talking chief, for if the ritual were performed and the bride proved 'not to be a virgin', then all of the old women of her family would 'beat and berate her'.

Napoleone's account of February 1926 made it plain, furthermore, that this custom applied not only to the *taupou,* but to 'ordinary marriages' as well. His account also made it clear that with their ritual of public defloration at marriage — a ritual that traditionally applied to 'ordinary marriages' as well as to that of the *taupou* — the Samoans were much preoccupied with female virginity. This information fully confirmed all that Mead had been told by Helen Wilson in Leone on 10 October 1925 and by To'aga, the wife of Sotoa the high chief of Luma, on 16 December 1925. By March 1926, then, Mead had been repeatedly informed about the sexual mores of the Samoans.

By 7 March 1926 Mead had still made no systematic investigation of the sexual behaviour of the adolescent girls she was supposed to be studying. Instead, she had been giving her time to ethnological research for the Bishop Museum, and on 8 March 1926, when a whale-boat arrived from the off-lying island of Ofu, Mead, 'lured by thoughts of ethnological gain', at once hired it to take her there for a ten-day visit. Her aim was to complete her ethnology of Manu'a for the Bishop Museum. Once again, Mead was abandoning research on her adolescent girls, none of whom could be contacted from Ofu or Olosega.

In her letter to Boas of 15 February 1926, Mead listed the information on a range of aspects of the behaviour of adolescent girls that she was proposing to collect by the end of March 1926, after which there would still remain for 'special investigation' the 'sexual life' of the adolescent girl, as well as 'any philosophical conflicts' that might be evinced. These topics, Mead told Boas, were 'the most difficult to get at' and required 'the greatest facility in the language and the longest intimacy'. She was, therefore, deferring systematic research on the 'sexual life' of the adolescent girl and on 'any philosophical conflicts' until April 1926, the last month of her stay on Manu'a. Furthermore, in this letter to Boas of 15 February 1926 she once again recorded the preconception she had brought with her to Samoa, giving it as her opinion that in Manu'a there was 'great promiscuity between puberty and marriage'.

This then was the mistaken belief that Mead took with her on her journey to Ofu and Olosega, on which she was accompanied, as travelling companions, by two young women from Fitiuta, Fa'apua'a and Fofoa, who were a few months older than Mead herself. Mead, identified as she was with the US Navy, was, in effect, a member of the governing elite from America, and so was able to behave as she did, living, as she put it, 'like a visiting young village princess'. In particular, at the US Navy Commissary, Mead had access to resources quite beyond the reach of either Fa'apua'a or Fofoa. Subordinate though they were to their American benefactor, Fa'apua'a and Fofoa were, nonetheless, thoroughly enjoying themselves. They were having a holiday together with all expenses paid.

When they went to wash Mead's clothes, they would always take along the ukuleles they had brought with them. In the mornings, before getting up, they would sing songs together.

In Samoa in the 1920s, it was unusual for unescorted females to travel about together. The arrival in Ofu village of three young women, one of them an American with a Samoan *taupou* title, aroused intense interest. On the second night of their stay, Mead, Fa'apua'a and Fofoa were ceremonially courted by the *aumaga* of Ofu, made up entirely of untitled men, most of them unmarried. On such occasions, which are called *aiava*, there is much speech making, singing and dancing, with first one side performing and then the other. There is also, during *aiava* of this kind, a great deal of light-hearted banter, frequently involving sexual innuendoes and allusions. Fa'apua'a recollected that during their meeting with the *aumaga* of Ofu, she and Fofoa joked with Mead, asking if there was a voting man she especially fancied and that when Mead jokingly replied that indeed there was, they bantered with her about the choice she had made. According to Fa'apua'a, it was on the island of Olosega, on 11 March 1926, the day following this formal but agreeably titillating encounter with the high-spirited young men of Ofu, that Mead, with whom they had already begun to joke about erotic matters, first began to question them concerning the sexual behaviour of the girls of Manu'a.

On 13 March 1926, after having completed her ethnological enquiries on the island of Olosega, Mead, accompanied by Fa'apua'a and Fofoa, walked all the way back to Ofu village. It was an experience that Mead described as 'sheer delight'. From the western tip of the island of Olosega they were ferried one at a time by outrigger canoe to the eastern end of the island of Ofu. From there, the three of them made their way along the southern coast of Ofu back to the village in which they had been staying earlier. It was, as Mead describes it, 'a long walk skirting the sea, at places racing the tide or leaping between high waves from one wet rock to another, but mostly following an easy trail, under a weak, complacent sun'. According to Fa'apua'a it was during this 'long walk' when Fa'apua'a and Fofoa were alone with her that Mead questioned them closely about sexual behaviour.

Since writing to Boas on 15 February about the research she intended to do on her sample of adolescent girls, virtually all of Mead's time, except for bulletin and letter writing, had been given to ethnological research, first in Fitiuta and then on Ofu and Olosega, locations far removed from the villages of Luma, Si'ufaga and Faleasao where all of the adolescent girls she was supposed to be studying lived. Indeed, by 13 March 1926, well over half of the time that Mead had allowed for the collection of the mass of information listed in her letter to Boas of 15 February had passed without her making any progress at all. And there still remained to be tackled, in April 1926, her 'special investigation' of the sexual behaviour of Samoan girls, when she would be systematically investigating this topic for the first time. Because of the great amount of time she had given to ethnological research, there was an immense amount to be done — and very little time in which to do it. Thus, by 13 March 1926, the 'investigation of the adolescent girl' as 'a study in heredity and environment', which she was in Samoa to undertake at the express wish and under the direct supervision of Professor Franz Boas, was in a state of considerable crisis. It was a crisis that had been created because, in Mead's own words, she had 'abandoned' her interest in 'socially unimportant adolescents' for almost a month in order to do quite unrelated research for her projected monograph on the ethnology of Manu'a. It was in this impasse that Mead turned to the questioning of her travelling companions about sexual behaviour, hoping that in this way she could make up for lost time, and, if at all possible, reach a solution to the research problem Boas had assigned to her.

It was on Saturday, 13 March 1926 then, when alone with Fa'apua'a and Fofoa for some hours, that Mead grasped the opportunity to question them. According to Fa'apua'a, Mead put to Fofoa and herself the preposterous proposition (so it seemed to them) that despite the great emphasis on virginity in the *fa'aSamoa* and within the Christian church of which all Manu'ans were adherents at that time, unmarried Samoan girls were, **in secret**, sexually promiscuous. In this way Mead was seeking to substantiate her preconception that in Samoa there was 'great promiscuity between puberty and marriage'.

If only she could obtain from Fa'apua'a and Fofoa a clear confirmation concerning the premarital promiscuity that she believed secretly existed in Manu'a, she would then have established a cultural pattern that would allow her to reach what she so desperately needed, an acceptable solution to the problem Boas required her to investigate under the terms of her research fellowship. She had been led to believe by Boas that informants like Fa'apua'a and Fofoa could speak for the culture by which they had been shaped.

In Samoa, it is not acceptable, in ordinary conversation, 'to discuss sexual matters publically'. And so, in their embarrassment at Mead's brashness, Fa'apua'a and Fofoa, having conspiratorially pinched one another, blandly agreed to all she had suggested to them, telling her with due embellishment that they, like other young women and girls, regularly spent their nights with members of the opposite sex. In so doing they were, as a prank, engaging in what Tim O'Meara has termed 'recreational lying' which is 'one of the main forms of entertainment' among Samoans. It is also a custom that is very much a part of Samoan culture.

Called *ula, tausua, taufa'alili* or *taufa'ase'e* (depending on the intentions of the perpetrators), 'recreational lying', as O'Meara has noted, 'happens continually' in Samoa, with all ages engaging in it, people tell you stories 'especially about sex', try to get you to believe them, and then 'sort of chuckle inside'. As this account of O'Meara's indicates, the 'recreational lying' that is so common among Samoans is a form of behaviour in which, in the words of Curtis MacDougall, 'a deliberately concocted untruth' is made to 'masquerade' as the truth, this being MacDougall's definition of a hoax. In the *Shorter Oxford English Dictionary*, a hoax is defined as 'a humorous or mischievous deception with which the credulity of the victim is imposed upon', with the term hoax being derived from the Latin *iocus*, meaning to joke or jest. The terms that Samoans commonly use to describe or refer to this behaviour clearly demonstrate that we are dealing with a form of joking behaviour. Thus, whereas *ula* (the term that the late Galea'i Poumele used in his conversation with Fa'apua'a on 13 November 1987) means to make fun of someone, *tausua* (the term that Fa'apua'a used in her interviews with Unasa L.F. Va'a) means 'to joke'; *taufa'alili* (another term used by Fa'apua'a on 13 November 1987) means 'to cause someone to shake with laughter' and the meaning of *taufa'ase'e* is 'to deceive in a joking way' (lit. to cause someone to lose her footing). *Taufa'ase'e* behaviour is thus a culturally ordained form of joking behaviour quite different in its intention from outright lying.

This then was the quintessentially Samoan response that Fa'apua'a and Fofoa fell back on when Mead advanced what to them was the ludicrous notion that the adolescent girls of Manu'a were, in secret, sexually promiscuous. As Fa'apua'a remarked to the late Galea'i Poumele, when he interviewed her in Fitiuta on 13 November 1987, 'As you know, Samoan girls are terrific liars when it come to joking, but Margaret accepted our trumped up stories as though they were true.'

According to Fa'apua'a, she and Fofoa colluded in telling Mead what they did because of their embarrassment at her insistent questioning on the topic of sexuality. They were enjoying themselves like true Samoans at the expense of a visiting American. They had no idea that Mead was an anthropologist, who, having taken their untruths and hyperbole to be facts, would put them in a book. If only Mead had challenged them, Fa'apua'a commented, they would at once have admitted that they were only joking. But Mead never did challenge them.

Mead's hoaxing on 13 March 1926 is fully attested to by the sworn testimony of Fa'apua'a Fa'amu, which is of a kind that could be presented in any court of law. Furthermore, with quite decisive historical significance, Fa'apua'a's sworn testimony is fully confirmed by Mead's entirely independent account dating from 1931 of what went on between herself and Fa'apua'a and Fofoa on the island of Ofu in March of 1926. For the historian, this independent confirmation of a specific happening is like a fix in coastal navigation. It is evidence of quite conclusive relevance. We know that we are dealing with an historical reality.

The account, by Margaret Mead of the time she spent with Fa'apua'a and Fofoa on the islands of Ofu and Olosega in March of 1926, is contained in a little-known book entitled *All True! The Record of Actual Adventures That Have Happened to Ten Women of Today,* which was published in New York in 1931. The 'adventure' by 'Dr. Margaret Mead' is entitled 'Life as a Samoan Girl'. It begins with a reference to 'the group of reverend scientists' who sent her to study the adolescent girls of Samoa with 'no very clear idea' of how she was 'to do this'. It ends with an account of her journey with Fa'apua'a and Fofoa to the islands of Ofu and Olosega in March 1926. Mead, using pseudonyms, refers to Fa'apua'a and Fofoa as the 'two Samoan girls. Braided Roses and Born-in-Three-Houses', and she describes how these 'two Samoan girls' (in fact they were both 24 years of age and slightly older than Mead herself) accepted the 'great squares' of bark cloth that were presented to her after she had, on Ofu, danced as a ceremonial virgin. Mead then records the crucially significant information that: 'In all things I had behaved as a Samoan, for only so, only by losing my identity as far as possible, had I been able to become acquainted with the Samoan girls, receive their whispered confidences and learn at the same time the answer to the scientists' questions'. Here Mead is specifically linking the 'whispered confidences' of Fa'apua'a and Fofoa (which we know, from the sworn testimony of Fa'apua'a, were about the sexual mores of the Samoans) to her being able to obtain an 'answer to the scientists' questions'. There could be no more explicit account of what in fact had happened!

It should be noted that Meads use of the information provided by Fa'apua'a and Fofoa was perfectly sincere, for a hoaxed individual is quite oblivious of what it is that has happened. Indeed, all of Mead's attitudes in respect of Samoa from mid-March 1926 onward must be assessed in the light of this fundamental psychological fact. Her letter to Boas dated Ofu, 14 March 1926, her book *Coming of Age in Samoa* of 1928, and everything she subsequently wrote on Samoa were written in a complete lack of awareness that she had on Saturday, 13 March 1926, been comprehensively hoaxed about the sexual mores of the Samoans.

The independent accounts of Fa'apua'a and of Mead herself are also fully corroborated by the highly revealing letter that Mead wrote to Franz Boas in Ofu village on Sunday, 14 March 1926. This letter is a document of crucial historical significance. In her letter to Boas of 15 February 1926, Mead, in addition to listing the wide range of information she was planning to collect on her sample of adolescent girls, informed him that she was deferring systematic research on the 'sexual life' of the adolescent girl until April 1926, the last month of her stay in Manu'a. On 20 February 1926 she travelled to Fitiuta to work on her 'ethnology of Manu'a' for the Bishop Museum, and this was followed, on 8 March 1926, by her ethnological expedition to the island of Ofu and Olosega. In giving her time to the 'ethnology of Manu'a' in this way, Mead was completely abandoning the study of her sample of adolescent girls, all of whom resided in three villages at the western end of the island of Ta'u, Luma, Si'ufaga and Faleasao. Yet, in her letter to Boas of 14 March 1926, Mead informed him that 'her problem' was 'practically completed', and at once proceeded to summarise her 'results'. 'Sexual life' (i.e. the 'sexual life' of the adolescent Samoan girl), she informed Boas, 'begins with puberty in most cases', adding that 'fairly promiscuous intercourse obtains until marriage'.

This information cannot possibly have come from Mead's study of her sample of adolescent girls for she had, on 14 March, not undertaken the 'special investigation' of the 'sexual life' of the adolescent girl that was planned for April 1926. It is thus information that can only have come from the 'whispered confidences' of Fa'apua'a and Fofoa on the previous day. The 'whispered confidences' of Fa'apua'a and Fofoa had convinced

Mead of the 'truth' of her belief that, in secret, the unmarried females of Manu'a were sexually promiscuous and it was on this entirely mistaken opinion that she based her conclusion that, because the community did not attempt to 'curb' this promiscuity, there was an absence of stress.

It was in this way then that Mead, on 14 March 1926, solved the problem she had been set by Boas. During a brief return visit to Samoa in November 1971, Mead confessed that it was a problem she 'didn't even want to study'. What the 'whispered confidences' of Fa'apua'a and Fofoa had done was to provide her with a solution she could present to Boas. She was however completely ignoring what she had been told about the sexual mores of Samoa by Helen Wilson, To'aga and Napoleone. She had thus really done no more than reach a result that would, she felt, please Boas, whose approval she so greatly desired.

When Mead's letter of 14 March 1926 reached New York, Boas was indeed pleased and at once wrote to her. Addressing her as 'My dear Flower of Heaven', he told her how glad he was that she had been able to 'do so well' with her 'difficult problem' as to 'feel able' to state her results 'so succinctly'. Boas, given his own beliefs, had found Mead's mistaken 'results' to be entirely acceptable.

A great deal of highly significant historical evidence is also revealed in the actions that Mead took after she had announced to Boas in her letter of 14 March, her answer to his problem. Mead had asked Boas in January 1926: 'If I simply write conclusions and use my cases as illustrative material will it be acceptable?' When she wrote to him on 14 March 1926, Mead was awaiting 'with great interest' Boas's reply to this pivotal question. She was still on the island of Ofu when Boas's letter of 15 February reached her on 11 March 1926. He had answered her momentous question in the affirmative, thus granting her the option to 'simply write conclusions' and to use 'cases' as 'illustrative material'. This answer marked a crucially significant turning point in Mead's fieldwork in Manu'a.

From her questioning of Fa'apua'a and Fofoa she had identified, she was convinced, the covert pattern of adolescent sexual behaviour in Samoa, and had formally announced her 'results' in her letter to Boas of 14 March 1926. This meant, as far as Mead was concerned, that she had successfully provided Boas with the 'sort of thing' that she understood he 'wanted', and with this conclusion concerning a topic that she 'didn't even want to study', she did no further research at all on the 'sexual life' of the adolescent girl.

Indeed, as soon as she got back to the US Naval Dispensary on the island of Ta'u, Mead wrote to Boas again. After receiving his letter of 15 February 'on presentation of results', she had decided, she told him in a hurried note, written on 19 March 1926, to 'finish up' her work 'in the next month' and to terminate her fieldwork a month earlier than planned.

In her 'plan of research' submitted to the Board of National Research Fellowships in the Biological Sciences in February 1925 Mead had written of spending 'a year of actual fieldwork in Samoa'. In Samoa, in her report to the National Research Council of 6 January 1926, she proposed five months of 'intensive study of the adolescent girl', in addition to the four weeks of inquiry she had completed in 1925. This would have meant a total of six months of fieldwork in Manu'a. To achieve this, she would have had to continue her research in Manu'a until early in June 1926, when she would have been entitled to 'six weeks' vacation. But from 19 March onwards she was intent on leaving Manu'a and heading for the south of France just as soon as she possibly could. The 'blue honey of the Mediterranean', as F. Scott Fitzgerald called it, was beckoning. By terminating her fieldwork in Manu'a in April, she could sail from American Samoa for Australia on 10 May 1926, and reach Marseilles on 25 June 1926 for a protracted holiday in France, England and Italy.

This sudden cutting short of her fieldwork in Manu'a by over a month had drastic consequences for her projected 'special investigation' of the 'sexual life' of the adolescent girl, which, as she had informed Boas in her letter to him of 15 February, she was due to undertake during the month of April 1926. The last entry of 24 March 1926 in her loose-leaf folder is headed 'Cases To Use as Illustrations' and clearly establishes that she had adopted Boas's acceptance or her proposal of January 1926 that she should 'simply write conclusions', and use 'cases as illustrative material'. And, how did she spend the time while awaiting the arrival of the US Navy vessel in which she would leave Manu'a? As recorded in her bulletin of 24 March 1926, she spent the time that was left to her on the island of Ta'u in patching such 'holes' in her ethnology of Manu'a as 'the width of a basket, the height of a post, the name of a feast, how they burn scars, what you really call your mother's brother, and how many fires there were at a death feast'.

In view of the fact that the information she had been given by Helen Wilson, To'aga and Napoleone about the sexual mores of the Samoans, involving, as it did, ritual defloration in public at marriage, there was, in scientific terms, an imperative need to carry out the 'special investigation' of the 'sexual life' of the adolescent girl that she had planned for April 1926. What was needed was a detailed testing of her statement to Boas, in her letter of 14 March 1926, that in Manu'a 'sexual life begins with puberty in most cases' and that 'fairly promiscuous intercourse obtains until marriage'. Yet, as the relevant historical documents show, after she had dispatched her letter of 14 March 1926 to Boas in New York, Mead engaged in no further systematic investigation of the sexual behaviour of adolescent girls. As far as she was concerned, the problem that Boas had imposed upon her and that she 'didn't even want to study', had already been answered in a way that Boas would find 'acceptable'.

And so, the 'special investigation' of the 'sexual life' of the adolescent girl that had to be carried out during April of 1926, if Margaret Mead's researches in Samoa were to have any genuinely scientific significance, was never undertaken. By the first week of April, when she should have been carrying out this crucially important investigation, her days were 'simply a procession of ceremonial farewells'. Indeed, with 'so little left to do', there was even time, as she mentioned on 7 April 1926, in a letter to her grandmother, for her to write a short story about the faraway valley in rural Pennsylvania where she herself had come of age. It was a story entitled 'The Conscientious Myth Maker'. By 16 April she was back in Pago Pago en route to the south of France.

Thus, at no stage during her five-month stay in Manu'a did Margaret Mead carry out a systematic investigation of the sexual lives of her sample of adolescent girls. Instead, the results contained in her letter to Boas of 14 March 1926 were obtained from the apparent confirmation by Fa'apua'a and Fofoa of her false belief that in Samoa there was 'great promiscuity between puberty and marriage'. That Mead failed to carry out, during April 1926, her planned 'special investigation' of the 'sexual life' of the adolescent girl is, in scientific terms, a scandal, of a kind unique in the history of 20th century anthropology. It means that the conclusions about sexual behaviour that Mead reached in *Coming of Age in Samoa* are, demonstrably, not based on any kind of systematic empirical investigation. This undeniable historical fact impugns, in the most basic way, the Samoan fieldwork of the 24-year-old Margaret Mead.

Mead's official report was entitled 'The Adolescent Girl in Samoa'. After Franz Boas had pronounced himself 'completely satisfied' with it, it was dispatched on 14 April 1927 to the National Research Council of the USA and, on 10 May 1927, approved for publication as *Coming of Age in Samoa.*

In this report, Mead says of the adolescent girl that 'all of her interest' is 'expended on clandestine sex adventures'. She also lists living as a girl 'with many lovers as long as possible' as one of 'the uniform and satisfying ambitions' of the Samoan girl. In *Coming of Age in Samoa* she writes of the deferring of marriage 'through as many years of casual love-making as possible'. To this mistaken view of Samoa Margaret Mead adhered for the rest of her life. Thus, in 1950 she described Samoa as one of the 'best studied examples' of 'premarital freedom'. It was certainly her belief on 10 November 1964, when she visited me in the Research School of Pacific Studies of The Australian National University in Canberra. During a major interview published some two years before her death in 1978, she was still attributing the easy nature of adolescence in Samoa to 'freedom of sex'. All of these generalisations about 'premarital promiscuity' in Samoa are entirely in accord with the letter Mead wrote to Boas on 14 March 1926, the day after she had been hoaxed by Fa'apua'a and Fofoa — a hoaxing which gave rise to what may be properly called 'the Mead myth' about Samoa.

According to Mead, Franz Boas thought that her study of adolescents in Samoa 'would indicate that culture is very important', and when, in Chapter 13 of *Coming of Age in Samoa,* she proclaimed 'cultural conditioning' to be all important, Franz Boas accepted this conclusion with alacrity. Thus, not only did Boas vouch for *Coming of Age in Samoa* as a 'painstaking investigation', but in discussing Mead's Samoan research in his book *Anthropology and Modern Life* of 1928, he repeated, as though it were a fully substantiated anthropological fact, Dr Margaret Mead's entirely false claim that in Samoa, where there was 'freedom of sexual life', the 'adolescent crisis disappears'.

It so happens that 1927 was the year when, during a visit to New York, Jacob Epstein sculpted a portrait of Franz Boas. Boas's face, according to Epstein, was 'scarred and criss-crossed with mementos of the many duels of his student days in Heidelberg, but what was still left whole in his face was as spirited as a fighting cock'. While engaged in the nature–nurture controversy, Boas had been fighting for well over a decade to establish his belief in 'the complete molding' of human behaviour 'by social conditioning'. When Margaret Mead presented him with an apparent proof of this belief he was overjoyed. As Liam Hudson and Bernadine Jacot have put it, 'What Mead showed Boas was what he wanted to see and having seen what he wanted to see, considerations of science and scholarship went by the board.' Convinced, as he was, of the 'truth' of his ideas, all that mattered to him was that he had 'won'. That Boas behaved in this highly partisan way shows how eager he was to promote the idealist ideology of which for decades he had been a prominent advocate. Most certainly, Boas's active promotion of Margaret Mead's *Coming of Age in Samoa* as a 'painstaking investigation' was crucial in securing its widespread acceptance by anthropologists and others as 'careful scientific work', and, by George Spindler of Stanford University in 1978 (50 years after its first publication) as the 'epitome of anthropology'.

It is now known from detailed historical research that the extreme environmentalist conclusion to which the young Margaret Mead came in *Coming of Age in Samoa* is based on evidence that is quite unacceptable scientifically. Thus, *Coming of Age in Samoa,* far from being a 'scientific classic' (as Mead and Boas supposed), is in certain vital respects (as in its dream-like second chapter) a work of anthropological fiction. Indeed, the Intercollegiate Studies Institute of Wilmington, Delaware, in listing the 50 worst and best books of the century, has adjudged Margaret Mead's *Coming of Age in Samoa,* with its approving Foreword by Franz Boas, to be the 'very worst' book of the 20th century.

Furthermore, in the light or present-day knowledge it is also evident that Boasian culturalism at the beginning of the 21st century has become a scientifically unacceptable belief system. During the last half of the 20th century there were, in the words of Ernst Mayr, 'unprecedented breakthroughs in genetics, cellular biology and neuroscience'. Never before have there been such fundamental advances in our understanding of the mechanisms of life. Then, on 26 June 2000, came the announcement of the virtual completion of the Human Genome Project. It can thus be said, in the light of present-day knowledge, that Boas's declaration of the early 1930s (derived from Mead's general conclusion in *Coming of Age in Samoa*) that 'the genetic elements which may determine personality' are 'altogether irrelevant as compared with the powerful influence of the cultural environment' is one of the most egregious anthropological errors of all time.

In 1984, George Milner, who, when compiling his scholarly *Samoan Dictionary*, worked in all parts of the Samoan archipelago, judged that 'Mead's Samoan fieldwork was a disaster, and its data unreliable in the extreme'. Since that time, protracted and detailed historical research has fully vindicated Milner's judgement, Indeed, the historical evidence on Mead's Samoan fieldwork is now of a kind sufficient to convince any rational man or woman. There will, however, I have no doubt, always be a lunatic fringe of true believers, who will, while clinging to the wreckage of Boasian culturalism, persist in their efforts to reinstate Mead's aberrant conclusion of 1928.

For my part, I am satisfied with the detailed historical research that I have been able to conduct. And, having been able to withstand the irrational opprobrium that has been heaped upon me by the Meadophiles of the USA, I find solace in the tag: '*finis coronat opus*'. The controversy over Margaret Mead's Samoan fieldwork is then, for me, finally at an end.

References

GENERAL

1. The references to the sources on which this analysis is based can be found in: *Margaret Mead and Samoa — The Making and Unmaking of an Anthropological Myth* (Harvard University Press, 1983) and *The Fateful Hoaxing of Margaret Mead — A Historical Analysis of Her Samoan Research* (Westview Press, 2nd edition, 1999).

2. All of my Samoan papers, including my fieldnotes of the 1940s and the 1960s, together with the full record of the sworn testimony of Fa'apua'a Fa'amu have been lodged in the Special Collections Department of the Geisel Library of the University of California, San Diego.

Adams, G.

1928 'Human instincts', *American Mercury* 14:458.

Auden, W.H.

1966 'Vespers', in *Collected Shorter Poems, 1927–1957* (London, Faber and Faber), p.335.

Bateson, William

 Report of the Eighty-Fourth Meeting of the British Association for the Advancement of Science, Australia, 1914 (London, John Murray, 1915), pp.3–38; also published in *Nature* 93:635–642, 674–681), *Science* (40:287–302, 319–333), and in the *Annual Report* (for) *of the Smithsonian Institution* (Washington, Government Printing Office, 1916), pp.359–394.

1923 'The revolt against the teaching of evolution in the United States', *Nature* 112:313–314.

Beach, F.A.

1955   'Ontogeny and living systems', in *Group Processes, Transactions of the First Conference,* ed. B. Schaffner (New York, Josiah Macy Jr Foundation), p.14.

Boas, F.

1894   'Human faculty as determined by race', *Proceedings, American Association for the Advancement of Science* 43:218.

1911   *The Mind of Primitive Man* (New York, Macmillan), p.155.

1932   'The aims of anthropological research', *Science* 76:607.

Bonner, John Tyler

1980   *The Evolution of Culture in Animals.* Princeton: Princeton University Press.

Bouchard, Thomas, et al.

1990   Sources of Human Psychological Differences. The Minnesota Study of Twins Reared Apart. *Science* 250:223–228.

Breland, K. and M. Breland

1965   'The misbehavior of organisms', in *Readings in Animal Behavior,* ed. T.E. McGill (New York, Holt, Rinehart and Winston), p.459.

Bridger, W.H. and B. Birns

1968   'Experience and temperament in human neonates', in *Early Experience and Behaviour: the Psychobiology of Development,* ed. G. Newton and S. Levine (Springfield, Illinois, Charles C. Thomas), p.89.

Bronowski, J.

1965   *The Identity of Man* (New York, Natural History Press). p.100.

Brown, Donald

1991   *Human Universals,* New York: McGraw-Hill.

Burnham, J.C.

1968   'On the origins of behaviorism', *Journal of the History of the Behavioral Sciences* 4:143–151.

Calverton, V.F.

1924   'The rise of objective psychology', *Psychological Review* 31:426.

1927   'The analysis of behavior', *Modern Quarterly* 4:302.

Carter, G.S.

1957   *A Hundred Years of Evolution.* London: Sidgwick and Jackson, p.121.

Coghill, G.E.

1929   *Anatomy and the Problem of Behavior.* New York: Macmillan.

Conklin, E.G.

1930   *Heredity and Environment in the Development of Man,* rev. ed. (Princeton, University Press), p.72. (First edition was in February 1915).

Crick, F.

1966   *Of Molecules and Men* (Seattle and London, University of Washington Press), p.52.

Cuénot, L.

1922   'The inheritance of acquired characters', *Annual Report, Smithsonian Institution* (for the year ending 30 June 1921) (Washington, Government Printing Office), p.336.

Darwin. C.

1859   *The Origin of Species by Means of Natural Selection* (London, John Murray), p.488.

1868   *Variation of Animals and Plants under Domestication* (London, John Murray), Vol. 2, chapter xxvii.

Darwin, F. (ed.)

1888   *The Life and Letters of Charles Darwin* (London, John Murray), Vol. III, p.133.

de Beer, G.

1963   *Charles Darwin Evolution by Natural Selection* (London, Nelson), chapter 8.

Degler, Carl N.

1991   *In Search of Human Nature: The Decline and Revival of Darwinism in American Social Thought.* New York: Oxford University Press.

Delgado, J.M.R.

1963   'Cerebral heterostimulation in a monkey colony', *Science* 141:1613.

Diamond, Jared

1991   *The Rise and Fall of the Third Chimpanzee.* London: Radius.

Diamond, Marian C.

1988   *Enriching Heredity: The Impact of the Environment on the Anatomy of the Brain.* New York: Free Press.

Dobzhansky, T.

1964   *Heredity and the Nature of Man* (New York, Harcourt, Brace and World), p.55.

1967   'Of flies and man', *American Psychologist* 22:42.

Döhl, J.

1969   Versuche mit einer Schimpansin über Abkürzungen bei Umwegen mit selbständigen Zwischenzielen. *Zeitschrift fur Tierpsychologie* 26:200–207.

Dubos, R.J.

1968   *So Human an Animal* (New York, Scribner), p.77.

Dunn, Judy and Robert Plomin

1990   *Separate Lives: Why Siblings are so Different.* New York: Basic Books.

Durkheim, E.

1895   *Les règles de la méthode sociologique* (Paris).

Eibl-Eibesfeldt, Irenius

1989   *Human Ethology.* London: Aldine de Gruyter.

Fantz, R.L.

1961   'The origin of form perception', *Scientific American* 204(5):66–72.

Fisher, R.A.

1918   'The correlations between relatives on the supposition of Mendelian inheritance', *Transactions, Royal Society of Edinburgh* 52:399–433.

Foxx, R.M.

1972   Attack preferences of the red-bellied piranha (*Serrasalmus nattereri*). *Animal Behaviour* 20:280–283.

Freeman, Derek

1970   *Report on the Iban.* London: The Athlone Press.

1983   *Margaret Mead and Samoa: The Making and Unmaking of an Anthropological Myth.* Cambridge, MA: Harvard University Press.

1999   *The Fateful Hoaxing of Margaret Mead.* Boulder: Westview Press.

Fuller, J.L. and W.R. Thompson

1960   *Behavior Genetics* (New York, John Wiley), p.4.

Galambos, R.

1967   'Introduction: Brain correlates of learning', in *The Neurosciences: A study program,* Gardner C. Quarton et al. (eds) (New York: Rockefeller University Press), pp.637–642.

Galton, F.

1875   'The history of twins as a criterion of the relative powers of nature and nurture', *Journal of the Anthropological Institute* 5:391–406.

Gazzaniga, Michael

1985   *The Social Brain: Discovering the Networks of the Mind.* New York: Basic Books.

Goodall, Jane

1990   *Through a Window: My Thirty Years with the Chimpanzees of Gombe.* Boston: Houghton Mifflin.

Gottlieb, G.

1968   'Prenatal behavior in birds', *Quarterly Review of Biology* 43:148–174.

Greenfield, Patricia M. and Savage-Rumbaugh, Sue E.

1990   Grammatical combinations in Pan paniscus: Processes of learning and invention in the evolution and development of language, in *Language and Intelligence in Monkeys and Apes.* Sue T. Parker and Kathleen R. Gibson eds. (Cambridge: Cambridge University Press), pp.540–578.

Gruter, Margaret

1991   *Law and the Mind: Biological Origins of Behavior.* Newbury Park: Sage.

Haeckel, E.

1877   'Title', *Nature* 16:491.

1879   *Freedom in Science and Teaching* (London, Kegan Paul), p.7.

1909   'Charles Darwin as an anthropologist', in *Darwin and Modern Science,* ed. A.C. Seward (Cambridge: Cambridge University Press), p.145.

Haldane, J.B.S.

1924   'A mathematical theory of natural and artificial selection. Part II', *Proceedings of the Cambridge Philosophical Society: Biological Science,* Vol. 1, pp.158–163.

1932   *The Causes of Evolution* (London, Longmans Green), pp.171–215.

1957   'The cost of natural selection', *Journal of Genetics* 55:511.

Harris, M.

1968   *The Rise of Anthropological Theory* (London, Routledge and Kegan Paul), p.15.

Heath, R.G.

1964   'Pleasure response of human subjects to direct stimulation of
        the brain: physiologic and psychodynamic considerations',
        in *The Role of Pleasure in Behavior,* ed. R.G. Heath (New York,
        Hoeber Medical Division), pp.219–243.

Herrick, C.J.

1967   cited by Robert B. Livingston, 'Introduction: Brain Circuitry
        relating to Complex Behavior' in *The Neurosciences,* p.500.

Hill, W.F and N.I. Spear

1963   'Choice between magnitudes of reward in a T maze', *Journal
        of Comparative and Physiological Psychology* 56:723–726.

Hirsch, J.

1963   'Behavior genetics and individuality understood'.
        Science 142:1437.

Hockett, C.F.

1967   Review of *Biological Foundations of Language* by E.H.
        Lenneberg, *Scientific American* 217(5):142.

Hodges, H.A.

1952   *The Philosophy of Wilhelm Dilthey* (London, Routledge
        and Kegan Paul), pp.312ff.

Hughes. B.O.

1975   'Spacial preference in the domestic hen'. *British Veterinary
        Journal* 131:563.

Huxley, Julian

1942   *Evolution: the Modern Synthesis* (London, George Allen and
        Unwin), p.28.

Huxley, T.H.

1880   'The coming of age of the Origin of Species', *Nature* 22:4.

Jay, P.

1963   'Mother–infant relations in langurs', in *Maternal Behaviour in
        Mammals,* ed. H. Rheingold (New York, John Wiley), p.286.

Jeffrey, E.C.

1925 'Drosophila and the mutation hypothesis', *Science* 62:3–5.

Jennings, H.S.

1917 'Observed changes in hereditary characters in relation to evolution', *Journal of the Washington Academy of Sciences* 7:283.

Johannsen, W.

1909 *Elemente der exakten Erblichkeit* (Jena, Fischer).

Kantor, J.R.

1921 'An attempt toward a naturalistic description of emotions'. *Psychological Review* 28:131.

1924 *Principles of Psychology* (New York, Knopf), p.172.

Kawai, M.

1965 'Japanese monkeys and the origin of culture', *Animals* 5:450–455.

Kellog, W.N.

1968 'Communication and language in home-raised chimpanzees'. *Science* 162:423–426.

Kennedy, J.M. and B.A. Baldwin

1972 Taste preferences in pigs for nutritive and non-nutritive sweet solutions. *Animal Behaviour* 20:706–718.

Kluback, W.

1956 *Wilhelm Dilthey's Philosophy of History* (New York, Columbia University Press), pp.103ff.

Kluckhohn C. and O. Prufer

1959 'Influences during the formative years', in *The Anthropology of Franz Boas,* ed. W. Goldschmidt (American Anthropological Association, Memoir No. 89). pp.9ff.

Kortlandt, A.

1966 'On tool-use among primates', *Current Anthropology* 7:215–216.

Kortlandt, A. and M. Kooij

1963   'Protohominid behaviour in primates'. *Symposia of the Zoological Society of London* 10:61–88.

Koshland, Daniel E. Jr

1987   Nature, Nurture and Behavior. *Science* 325:1445.

Kroeber, A.L.

1910   'The morals of uncivilized people'. *American Anthropologist* 12:437.

1915   'Eighteen professions', *American Anthropologist* 17:283–288.

1916   'Inheritance by magic', *American Anthropologist* 18:34.

1917   'The superorganic', *American Anthropologist* 19:163–213.

Lashley, K.E.

1926   'The relation between cerebral mass, learning and retention', *Journal of Comparative Neurology* 41:1–58.

Leakey, L.S.B.

1967   'Development of aggression as a factor in early human and pre-human evolution', in *Aggression and Defense (Brain Function.* Vol. 5) (Berkeley and Los Angeles, University of California Press), p.7.

Lenneberg, E.H.

1967   *Biological Foundations of Language* (New York, John Wiley), p.28 and pp.128ff.

Libet, Benjamin

1985   Unconscious cerebral initiative and the role of conscious will in voluntary action. *Behavioural and Brain Sciences* 8:529–566.

Lindsley, D.B.

1963   *Brain Function,* ed. C.D. Clernente and D.B. Lindsley (Berkeley and Los Angeles, University of California Press), 5:73ff.

Lorenz, K.

1935   'Companionship in bird life', reprinted in *Instinctive Behavior,* ed. C.H. Schiller (London, Methuen, 1957), pp.83–128.

Lorenz, K.

1955   'Morphology and behavior patterns in closely allied species', in *Group Processes, Transactions of the First Conference,* ed. B. Schaffner (New York, Josiah Macy Jr Foundation), p.183.

Lumsden, Charles J. and Wilson, Edward O.

1983   *Promethean Fire: Reflections on the Origin of Mind.* Cambridge, MA: Harvard University Press.

MacLean, Paul D.

1962   'New findings relevant to the evolution of psychosexual functions of the brain', *Journal of Nervous and Mental Disease* 135:289–301.

1990   *The Triune Brain in Evolution.* London: Plenum Press.

Manning, A.

1965   'Drosophila and the evolution of behaviour', in *Viewpoints in Biology,* ed. J.D. Carthy and C.L. Duddington (London, Butterworths), 4:126.

Mayr, E.

1959   'Where are we?', *Cold Spring Harbor Symposia on Quantative Biology* 24:1ff.

1963   *Animal Species and Evolution* (Cambridge, Mass., Harvard University Press), p.1.

Mead, Margaret

1928   *Coming of Age in Samoa.* New York: William Morrow.

1930   'Growing up in New Guinea', in *From the South Seas* (New York, Morrow, 1939), p.212.

Morgan, T.H.

1916   *A Critique of the Theory of Evolution.* Princeton: Princeton University Press.

Muller, H.J.

1965   'Means and aims of human genetic betterment', in *The Control of Human Heredity and Evolution,* ed. T.M. Sonneborn (New York, Macmillan), p.101.

1967   'The gene material as the initiator and the organizing basis of life', in *Heritage from Mendel,* ed. R.A. Brink (Madison, University of Wisconsin Press), p.443.

Osborn, H.F.

1922   'William Bateson on Darwinism', *Science* 55:194–197.

Passingham, Richard

1982   *The Human Primate.* Oxford: W.H. Freeman.

Pearson, K.

1914   *The Life, Letters and Labours of Francis Galton* (Cambridge: Cambridge University Press), Vol. 1, p.vi: in preface dated Gallon Laboratory, 8 April 1914.

Penfield, W. and T. Rasmussen

1952   *The Cerebral Cortex of Man: a clinical study of localization of function.* New York: Macmillan.

Pfaffman, C.

1967   *Introduction to Neurophysiology and Emotion* (first of a series on Biology and Behavior, proceedings of a conference held under the auspices of the Russell Sage Foundation and the Rockefeller University), ed. David C. Glass (New York, Rockefeller University Press and Russell Sage Foundation), p.ix.

Plomin, Robert

1990   *Nature and Nurture: An Introduction to Human Behavioral Genetics.* Pacific Grove: Brooks-Cole.

Punnett, R.C.

1950   'The early days of genetics', *Heredity* 4:1–10.

Radin, P.

1939   'The mind of primitive man', *New Republic* 98:303.

Reynolds, Vernon

1980   *The Biology of Human Action.* Oxford: W.H. Freeman.

Sackett, G.R.

1966   'Monkeys reared in isolation with pictures as visual input: evidence for an innate releasing mechanism', *Science* 154:1468–1473.

Schmalhausen, S.D.

1928   *Why We Misbehave* (New York, Macauley), p.17.

Scott, J.P.

1963   'The process of primary socialization in canine and human infants', *Monograph of the Society for the Research into Child Development* 28:1–47.

Scott, J.P. and J.L. Fuller

1965   *Genetics and the Social Behavior of the Dog* (Chicago and London, Chicago University Press), chapter 4.

Seagrim, G., E. Hackett, and J.D. Freeman

1970   *Man and the New Biology,* Canberra: Australian National University Press.

Shakespeare, W.

1947   *The Tempest,* Act IV, Scene 1 in *Complete Works of William Shakespeare* (Blackwell: Odhams Press).

Sibley, C.G. and J.F. Ahlquist

1984   The phylogeny of the hominoid primates as indicated by DNA-DNA hybridization. *Journal of Molecular Evolution* 20:2–15.

Simpson, G.G., C.S. Pittendrigh and L.H. Tiffany

1957   *Life: an Introduction to Biology* (New York, Harcourt, Brace), p.434.

Sperry, R.W.

1958   'Physiological plasticity and brain circuit theory', in *Biological and Biochemical Bases of Behavior,* ed. H.F. Harlow and C.N. Woolsey (Madison, University of Wisconsin Press), pp.401–424.

Spier, L.

1943   'Franz Boas and some of his views', *Acta Americana* 1:108.

1959   'Some central elements in the legacy', in *The Anthropology of Franz Boas,* ed. W. Goldschmidt (American Anthropological Association, Memoir No. 89), p.146.

Spuhler, J.N.

1967   'Genetics and Child Development', in *Genetic Diversity and Human Behavior* (Chicago: Aldine Publishing Company), pp.171–186.

Stocking, G.

1968   *Race, Culture and Evolution* (New York, Free Press), p.138.

Stoddart, D. Michael

1990   *The Scented Ape: The Biology and Culture of Human Odour.* Cambridge: Cambridge University Press.

Sturtevant, A.H.

1965   *A History of Genetics* (New York, Harper and Row), chapter 17.

Tarte, R.D. and R.L. Snyder

1973   Some sources of variation in the bar-pressing versus freeloading phenomenon in rats. *Journal of Comparative and Physiological Psychology* 84:128–133.

Teitelbaum, P.

1967   'The biology of drive' in *The Neurosciences,* ed. G.C. Quarton, T. Melnechuk and F.O. Schmitt (New York, Rockefeller University Press), p.559.

Thoday, J.M.

1967   'Selection and genetic heterogeneity' in *Genetic Diversity and Human Behavior,* ed. J.N. Spuhler (Chicago, Aldine Publishing Co.), pp.89–98.

Thompson, W.R.

1957   'Influence of prenatal maternal anxiety on emotionality in young rats', *Science* 125:698–699.

Turner, Victor

1983   Body, brain and culture. *Zygon* 18:221–245.

Tsumori, A.

1967   'Newly acquired behavior in social interactions of Japanese monkeys', *Social Communication among Primates,* ed. S.A. Altman (Chicago and London, University of Chicago Press), pp.207–219.

Tylor, E.B.

1871   *Primitive Culture* (London. John Murray). p.2.

van Lawick-Goodall, J.

1968   'The behaviour of free-living chimpanzees in the Gombe stream reserve', *Animal Behaviour Monographs,* Vol. 1, Part 3, pp.222ff.

Virchow, R.

1877   'The liberty of science in the modern state', *Nature* 17:74 and 112.

von Holst, E.

1935   'Uber den Prozess der zentralnervösen Koordination', *Pflügers Arch. ges. Physiol.* 236:149–159.

von Holst, E. and U. von Saint Paul

1963   'On the functional organization of drives', *Animal Behaviour* 11:1–20.

Washburn, S.L.

1968   'Behavior and the origin of man'. *Rockefeller University Review,* January–February, p.17.

Watson J.B.

1913   'Psychology as the behaviorist views it', *Psychological Review* 20:158.

1925   *Behaviorism* (New York, Norton), p.74.

1926   'What is behaviorism?' *Harper's Magazine* 152:729.

1928   *Psychological Care of Infant and Child* (London, George Allen and Unwin), p.18.

1936   'Title', in *A History of Psychology in Autobiography,* ed. C. Murchison (Worcester Mass., Clark University Press), Vol. 3, pp.279ff.

Watson, J.B. et al.

1929   'Is man a machine?' *Forum* 82:265.

Weismann, A.

1893   *The Germ-plasm: a Theory of Heredity.* London: Walter Scott.

Weiss, P.A.

1950   'Experimental analysis of co-ordination by the disarrangement of central-peripheral relations', *Physiological Mechanisms in Animal Behavior: Symposia of the Society for Experimental Biology* (New York, Academic Press), 4:92–111.

White, L.

1967   'The historical roots of our ecologic crisis', *Science* 155:1207.

Willis, J.C.

1922   *Age and Area.* Cambridge: Cambridge University Press.

1923   'The inadequacy of the theory of natural selection as an explanation of the facts of geographical distribution and evolution', *Report of the Ninetieth Meeting of the British Association, for the Advancement of Science, Hull, 1922* (London, John Murray), p.399.

Winson, Jonathan

1986   *Brain and Psyche: The Biology of the Unconscious.* New York: Vintage Books.

Wright, S.

1931   'Evolution in Mendelian populations', *Genetics* 16:97–159.

Wright, S.

1968   *Evolution and the Genetics of Populations,* Vol. 1, Genetic and biometric foundations. Chicago and London: University of Chicago Press.

Yamada, M.

1963   'A study of the blood-relationship in the natural society of the
        Japanese macaque', *Primates* 4:43–65.

Young, J.Z.

1987   Choice, biological, pp.147–148 in *The. Oxford Companion
        to the Mind.* Richard L Gregory, ed. Oxford: Oxford
        University Press.

Zirkle, C.

1959   *Evolution, Marxian Biology and the Social Scene* (Philadelphia,
        University of Pennsylvania Press), p.447.

www.ingramcontent.com/pod-product-compliance
Lightning Source LLC
Chambersburg PA
CBHW060749240726
48664CB00009BA/1672